THE DRY LANDSCAPING HANDBOOK

BEAUTIFUL YARD IN SPITE OF A DROUGHT

JOSIE POWERS

CONTENTS

INTRODUCTION

" *"To build, to plant, whatever you intend, /To rear the column, or the arch to bend, /To swell the terrace, or to sink the grot; /In all, let Nature never be forgotten. "*

- Alexander Pope

These timeless words by Alexander Pope succinctly encapsulate the essence of landscape architecture—a symphony between man's intent and nature's consent, a harmonious interplay where human creativity flourishes within the constraints and gifts of the natural environment.

The irony, however, is stark as we delve into the practical aspects of this ideal. In an era where climate change impacts are no longer a distant warning but an everyday reality, maintaining a vibrant, verdant landscape is increasingly challenging. The effects of prolonged dry spells and recurring droughts pose significant obstacles, particularly in various U.S. states, where a picturesque lawn or garden is not just a luxury but an emblem of the American dream.

Imagine the arid regions of California or the dry spells in Michigan, where water has become a precious commodity. Each droplet counts and wasting it on maintaining lush landscapes seems like an extravagance few can afford. The brittle, brown remnants of what were once green pastures stand as silent testaments to the changing climate. And it's not just about aesthetics; drought-impacted landscapes have real repercussions on local ecosystems, property values, and our mental well-being.

If you are reading this book, you may have already encountered these problems. Perhaps your once-thriving garden now resembles a barren wasteland, or the dream of nurturing a green oasis in your backyard seems increasingly elusive amidst dry spells. You may have tried every trick in the book, only to watch helplessly as your treasured plants wilt under the scorching sun. You may be wondering if it's time to give up on your green dreams and accept the inevitability of the arid climate.

However, the catalyst that brought you to this book is not despair but hope. Hope is underscored by the conviction that if nature could adapt and evolve, so can we. That, armed with the right knowledge and techniques, we can reclaim our gardens from the grip of drought, that we can still create lush landscapes that are not just visually pleasing but also ecologically sustainable. And that's precisely what this book aims to provide.

Through a 3-P approach—prepare, plant, and preserve—this book will equip you with the tools to transform your drought-ridden landscape into a flourishing, resilient oasis. It will guide you through the process of understanding your unique landscape conditions, choosing plants that are naturally suited to withstand dry spells, and applying sustainable landscape-management practices to ensure long-term success.

Imagine looking out of your window to a vibrant garden, every plant thriving in its chosen spot, the entire landscape humming with the gentle symphony of a well-balanced ecosystem. Imagine being able to maintain this lush oasis with minimal water usage, in harmony with the local climate, and without resorting to harmful chemicals. This book is your roadmap to that future, a step-by-step guide to creating and maintaining resilient landscapes in an era of climate uncertainty.

As we journey through this book, my goal is to be your companion and guide, sharing my experiences and insights, drawing from a wealth of scientific research and age-old wisdom. As a seasoned landscape enthusiast, I have wrestled with the realities of dry spells and droughts and have discovered the transformative power of sustainable practices.

There is a saying that every gardener cultivates a dream, and in this book, my dream is to help you realize yours. So, whether you are a seasoned gardener struggling to adapt to changing climates or a novice just setting foot into the exciting world of landscaping, remember, this is not just a book: It's a testament to resilience, a manifesto for a sustainable future, and above all, a celebration of the enduring beauty of nature.

In the subsequent chapters, we embark on an exploration of the underlying science of soil, water, and plant relationships, illuminating the mysteries of root systems, photosynthesis, and transpiration. We delve into the rich biodiversity of plants, each unique in its ability to withstand droughts and each with its unique beauty to grace your landscape.

We will then move on to explore the essential practices of landscape management, a crucial component that often spells the difference between a flourishing garden and a failing one. From understanding pest control and weed management to mastering turfgrass selection and management, each topic is addressed in detail, laying out a blueprint for best management practices.

As you navigate through the labyrinth of landscaping, armed with this newfound knowledge, you will begin to see changes—the rose bush that resisted blooming will burst forth in a riot of colors, the stubborn patch of lawn will start sprouting tender green blades, the skeletal tree will begin to show signs of life. Bit by bit, as your landscape begins to transform, you will realize that this is not merely a physical transformation but a metaphysical journey that intertwines with the cycles of life itself.

Along this journey, you will be equipped with an array of practical tools. From a handy turf-pest damage-monitoring chart to a comprehensive list of drought-hardy plants, the appendices serve as quick references to assist you in your day-to-day gardening endeavors. You'll discover landscape design ideas, inspiring you to create your unique green space. And all this knowledge culminates in a holistic approach to landscape installation and maintenance practices for water conservation, an embodiment of the adage "think global, act local."

At the heart of this book is a deep reverence for nature and an unwavering belief in human ingenuity. It is inspired by the countless gardeners who, faced with the most unforgiving climates, have created landscapes that defy belief. And it is guided by the knowledge of scientists and practitioners who have dedicated their lives to unlocking the secrets of resilient landscapes.

As you leaf through the pages, my hope is that this book becomes more than a manual. Let it be a source of inspiration, a reminder that, in the face of climate change, the solution is not surrender but adaptation. Let it spark your creativity, challenge your preconceptions, and guide your efforts to create a resilient, beautiful landscape that is a testament to your resilience and ingenuity.

So, whether you have a small backyard that you wish to convert into a drought-resistant oasis or you're a professional landscape architect grappling with large-scale projects in drought-prone areas, this book is for you. It's for anyone who believes in the power of nature and the potential of human innovation.

As Alexander Pope once wrote, "In all, let Nature never be forgotten." Armed with this book, not only will you remember nature, but you'll also learn to work with it, transforming your landscapes into thriving ecosystems that embody the beauty and resilience of our natural world.

So, let's embark on this journey together: Let's embrace the challenges, celebrate the small victories, and, most importantly, let's grow—not just plants and landscapes, but our understanding, our resilience, and our capacity to create beauty even in the most challenging circumstances. Welcome to the world of sustainable, drought-resistant landscaping. Remember, it's not the destination but the journey that counts, and what an incredible journey this will be!

I hope this introduction sets the tone for an engaging, insightful, and transformative exploration of sustainable landscaping practices. Enjoy the journey!

1

SUSTAINABILITY IS THE GAME

Interdependence, recycling, partnership, flexibility, diversity, and as a result of all these, sustainability. Our survival depends on our ecological literacy, on understanding and living by these principles of ecology.

–Fritjof Capra

These profound words by Fritjof Capra emphasize the essence of the journey we are about to embark on in the coming pages of this book.

Imagine a world where every action we take, every choice we make, is in harmony with our environment, where human beings, nature, and the economy are in perfect balance. In a nutshell, that is what sustainability is all about. Now, how about we bring this notion down to your own backyard? The concept might seem grandiose, but sustainable gardening and landscaping can help us get closer to this harmonious world.

Picture your favorite patch of garden. What if I told you that every single shrub, tree, and flower you've cultivated, or the way you tend your soil, or even how you recycle garden waste, could potentially be part of a solution to one of humanity's most pressing challenges—sustainability? You might be a green thumb, a landscaping enthusiast, or someone merely wondering how to maintain a beautiful garden under the harsh constraints of drought, and yet, each one of you can play a part in this grand design.

"Sustainability" is not just a buzzword; it has been our age-old tradition—something that we may have forgotten in our race toward modernization. We draw its meaning from the Brundtland Commission's notion of "meeting the needs of the present without compromising the ability of future generations to meet their own needs" (United Nations, 2023). This beautifully sums up the three pillars of sustainability: environment, economy, and society.

So why the emphasis on sustainability, you might ask? Because our very survival depends on it. As we strive to create beautiful landscapes in our surroundings, it's equally essential that we ensure they are sustainable. Sustainable landscaping is a practical response to our environmental responsibilities. It reduces pollution, energy use, erosion, and stormwater runoff, conserves resources, and creates thriving ecosystems that invite local wildlife. The benefits are plentiful, from low maintenance and longer life to reduced water usage and minimal use of fertilizers and pesticides.

But how do we translate these high-sounding principles into our everyday gardening practices, especially in dry and drought-like regions? That's precisely the question we'll be exploring in the chapters to come.

By now, you should have a basic understanding of what sustainability is and why it's so important, both globally and at the personal level of your own garden. And if you're wondering how to take this sustainability from your garden to the larger landscape around you, hang tight because that's exactly where we're headed next.

Hold on to your gardening gloves, for we are about to embark on a green journey that goes beyond aesthetics and dives into a realm where every tree planted and every drop of water saved contributes to the larger picture of a sustainable world. You're not just a gardener or landscaper; you're a caretaker of our shared future. Let's make it a greener one, shall we?

Let's delve deeper into the principles of sustainable landscaping in our upcoming chapters. Welcome aboard to the enlightening journey of sustainability!

UNDERSTANDING SUSTAINABILITY

Sustainability is an integral concept that pertains to a balanced and harmonious interaction between humanity and nature. The core idea underlying this concept centers on fulfilling our current requirements while safeguarding the potential for future generations to fulfill their own necessities. As we seek to sustain our way of life, we must also strive to promote social development and preserve our environment.

Origins of Sustainability

The term "sustainability" gained significant prominence with the publication of the Brundtland Report ("Our Common Future") in 1987. This report, published by the United Nations, underlined the detrimental environmental consequences of economic development and globalization. It called for a balanced approach that would counteract the impacts of industrialization and population growth. It is from this standpoint that our modern understanding of sustainability originated.

Sustainable Gardening: An Achievable Goal

Though the idea of sustainable gardening might seem daunting initially, it is simpler and more feasible than it might appear. By adopting practices like integrated pest management (IPM), companion planting, using beneficial insects, and composting, gardeners can drastically reduce their reliance on synthetic products like pesticides and fertilizers. Not only does this make for healthier gardens, but it also contributes to the broader aim of environmental sustainability.

Taking Sustainability to the Realm of Landscaping

As our understanding of the environmental impact of our actions continues to deepen, sustainability has been pushed to the forefront of many industries, and landscaping is no exception. Sustainable landscaping involves a variety of design, construction, implementation, and management practices that aim to minimize environmental damage and enhance natural ecosystems. It also reduces waste and energy use and contributes positively to biodiversity and ecological health.

The Paradigm of Sustainable Landscaping

Sustainable landscaping is an all-encompassing term that goes beyond just planting trees or maintaining a lawn. It includes strategies that provide key elements required for a healthy landscape, such as appropriate plant selection, effective moisture control, and organic fertilization. Moreover, these strategies take into consideration the interconnection of all elements in an environment and aim for their harmonious coexistence.

Furthermore, sustainable landscaping, whether for residential or commercial properties, is based on understanding and working with local environmental conditions. For instance, growing native plants helps in reducing maintenance, water usage, and the need for synthetic fertilizers and pesticides while promoting biodiversity and reducing energy consumption. This approach is not only ecologically beneficial but economically viable, as it increases property values and reduces costs associated with irrigation and pest management.

From Millennium Development Goals to the United Nations' 2030 Agenda

Subsequently, in 2010, the United Nations established the Millennium Development Goals, providing a strategic roadmap for reducing hunger and poverty, improving health and education, advocating equality for all, and promoting environmental sustainability. This commitment has further evolved into the

UN's 2030 Agenda, a comprehensive plan that focuses on people, the planet, and prosperity, aiming to fortify universal peace and access to justice.

The Three Pillars of Sustainability

The concept of sustainability is founded upon three essential pillars: the preservation of the environment, the advancement of social well-being, and the promotion of economic growth.

Environmental Sustainability

Environmental sustainability emphasizes the protection and rational use of our natural resources. It is about realizing that our natural environment isn't an infinite resource bank. Elements such as environmental conservation, a shift toward renewable energy, water conservation, sustainable architecture, and a more eco-friendly lifestyle contribute to environmental sustainability.

Social Sustainability

Social sustainability focuses on fostering social development and promoting cohesion among diverse communities and cultures. This includes ensuring quality healthcare, education, and upholding equality and fairness for all.

Economic Sustainability

Economic sustainability, on the other hand, aims to drive economic growth that benefits everyone without causing harm to our environment. This encompasses endeavors spanning various sectors aimed at fostering a fair distribution of economic resources, which in turn bolsters progress across the other two pillars of sustainability.

The Interdependence of Sustainability Pillars

In essence, these three pillars of sustainability are interdependent, and resolving global challenges such as a changing climate and water scarcity necessitates a collective commitment to sustainable development.

The journey toward sustainability requires us to think long term, act responsibly, and constantly be mindful of our footprint. The decisions we make today will significantly impact the world of tomorrow.

WHAT IS SUSTAINABLE GARDENING?

In essence, sustainable gardening refers to the process of using environmentally friendly methods to cultivate and manage your garden. It stands as a testament to a gardener's commitment to "do no evil" to Earth and its inhabitants. It supports, preserves, and reinforces natural systems, offering nourishment to the local ecosystem. Although the term lacks a technical definition, sustainable gardening ultimately represents good environmental stewardship.

In practice, sustainable gardening does not necessarily mean avoiding pesticides altogether. We all occasionally deal with pesky aphids or dreaded powdery mildew. However, the goal is to minimize our dependence on chemical treatments and seek more natural, organic solutions to common garden challenges.

Integrated Pest Management

A scientific-sounding term, IPM essentially emphasizes starting with the least toxic remedy to handle garden problems. Instead of immediately resorting to chemical pesticides, IPM encourages gardeners to study, monitor, and then address pest issues with minimally invasive methods. As a result, it curbs the overuse of harmful substances, making it an effective technique for sustainable gardening.

Companion Planting

Companion planting is a time-honored method used by gardeners to maintain the health of their plants naturally. The idea is to grow certain plants together, where one plant serves to either repel pests or attract beneficial insects that help the companion plant thrive. This approach confuses pests and disrupts their lifecycle, helping maintain the balance of the garden's ecosystem.

Beneficial Insects

These little allies are critical for the well-being of our gardens. If attracting them naturally fails, one can purchase beneficial insects and introduce them to the garden. These insects serve as a form of biological pest control, reducing the need for artificial pesticides and supporting the garden's overall health.

Composting

Composting remains an invaluable tool in sustainable gardening. The practice of turning organic waste into a nutrient-rich soil conditioner not only recycles kitchen and garden waste but also nourishes plants, retains soil moisture, protects plant roots from temperature fluctuations, and aids in disease resistance.

ENVIRONMENTAL IMPACTS AND BENEFITS OF SUSTAINABLE LANDSCAPING

Landscaping traditionally has significant environmental impacts, especially in urban settings. These impacts include extensive water usage, chemical runoff, and soil degradation. However, sustainable landscaping offers a viable alternative to these challenges. Through the emphasis on environmentally friendly approaches like decreasing water consumption, minimizing the utilization of fertilizers and pesticides, and incorporating green waste, sustainable landscaping can contribute positively to the environment.

The environmental benefits of sustainable landscaping extend to less-tangible areas as well. For instance, creating habitats for native fauna and preserving local biodiversity can contribute to ecosystem health. Moreover, the longevity of these landscapes allows for the continuation of these benefits over a prolonged period, thus creating a sustained positive impact on the environment.

Sustainable Landscaping and Its Role in Environmental Stewardship

Landscape managers, contractors, and homeowners play a critical role in this shift toward sustainable landscaping. Their actions directly affect the environmental impact of their properties and can significantly contribute to reducing waste and pollution. Recycling and upcycling are key strategies in this approach, with landscape materials being repurposed and organic waste being composted to enhance soil health.

Ultimately, sustainable landscaping is about making conscious, informed decisions that respect the natural environment and enhance its ability to support life. It's about understanding the intrinsic value of our local ecosystems and acting in ways that support their health and longevity. Through sustainable landscaping, we can create beautiful, thriving environments that not only enrich our lives but also contribute to a healthier planet.

CONCLUSION

Sustainability is an essential concept that addresses the harmonious coexistence of humanity and nature. It ensures the fulfillment of the needs of both current and future generations while concurrently preserving our planet's resources and avoiding depletion. This intricate balance pivots on three integral pillars, all of which are interdependent and crucial to tackling global environmental issues. The shift toward sustainable practices is evident in varied sectors, with sustainable gardening and landscaping exemplifying eco-conscious stewardship. These fields encapsulate environmentally friendly practices and choices that reinforce and enhance natural systems. Not only do these practices foster healthier, more vibrant landscapes and gardens, but they also underscore the broader aim of environmental sustainability. They contribute positively to biodiversity, ecological health, and the reduction of waste and energy use. Therefore, sustainable practices, from gardening to landscaping, form part of a broader endeavor to respect, conserve, and cultivate our planet.

2.

THE CORE PRINCIPLES

" *This is the fundamental idea underlying an ecological civilization: using nature's own design principles to reimagine the basis of our civilization. Changing our civilization's operating system to one that naturally leads to life-affirming policies and practices rather than rampant extraction and devastation.*

–Jeremy Lent

Jeremy Lent's words embody our path in this chapter as we delve into the principles of sustainable landscaping, the essence of our new ecological civilization. The one that thrives on the balance between humanity's advancements and the flourishing health of our natural world.

You might be looking out at your garden, parched under a merciless summer sun, and thinking, *How can I morph this into a lush oasis that not only flourishes in these dry conditions but also helps the environment?* Perhaps your lawn is already green, but you're noticing the strain on your resources—water, money, and time—as you constantly fight against the natural arid conditions. Either way, you've come to the right place.

You see, sustainable landscaping is not just about choosing a couple of hardy plants and hoping for the best. It is about developing an understanding of the land, the soil, and the natural ecosystems that once thrived in your local area. It's about leveraging these understandings to build landscapes that are resilient, beautiful, and synergistic with nature.

Let's imagine this scenario. Remember the last time you went hiking: Recall the green of the trees, the murmur of the brook nearby, and the vibrant colors of wildflowers nestling in the grass, all of them thriving without any gardener's attention. The secret? Nature's own design principles. We're about to explore those principles and how they can guide us in creating a stunning landscape that not only survives but thrives without an undue strain on resources.

As we venture into this realm of thoughtfully nurturing our green spaces, we will explore key principles that include recognizing water as a valuable resource, emphasizing the importance of soil conservation, preserving existing plant life, and practicing responsible management of material resources. Each of these principles forms the building blocks of a landscape that naturally resists drought, requires less maintenance, and provides a haven for local wildlife.

Let's not shy away from the obvious. This can sound quite daunting. Between selecting the right native plants, planning your garden beds, tackling water runoff challenges, and even managing pests, there's a lot to consider. But don't worry. I'm not leaving you to traverse this journey alone.

I've developed a unique approach to simplify the process. Enter the 3 Ps of drought landscaping: prepare, plant, and preserve. Understand these three elements, apply them diligently, and you'll be able to turn your backyard into a self-sustaining ecosystem that requires less upkeep, consumes fewer resources, and yet leaves a lasting impression on everyone who sets their eyes on it.

Remember, the journey toward a sustainable landscape is not a race. It's more of a hike, where every step brings a new understanding and a new appreciation for the world around us. So, let's get our boots dirty, roll up our sleeves, and step into the wonderful world of sustainable landscaping together.

DROUGHT LANDSCAPING, À LA SUSTAINABILITY

In the face of increasing environmental pressures, drought landscaping has emerged as a key strategy in sustainability, fusing ecology, design, and culture into a harmonious whole. Its principles are based on the concept of working with nature instead of against it, creating beautiful and practical landscapes that utilize precious resources like water and soil efficiently, conserve materials, and preserve existing plants. Through the strategic application of these principles, homeowners and urban developers alike can contribute significantly to environmental sustainability.

Understanding Drought Landscaping

Drought landscaping, also known as xeriscaping, primarily focuses on water conservation in landscaping design. As the name suggests, it is particularly beneficial in drought-prone regions but can be applied anywhere for increased sustainability. It emphasizes native over non-native species, promotes soil health, and minimizes the use of artificial inputs such as fertilizers and pesticides.

Principle #1—Treat Water as a Resource

Water is not an infinite resource, and with climate change, its scarcity is a looming issue worldwide. Drought landscaping seeks to address this problem directly. Through strategies like the use of native plants adapted to local rainfall conditions, the installation of water-efficient irrigation systems, and the incorporation of water-absorbing landscape features like rain gardens and bioswales, we can drastically reduce water consumption in our gardens and landscapes.

Principle #2—Value Your Soil

Healthy soil is a precious resource, teeming with life and packed with nutrients. Understanding your soil type, pH, and nutrient levels is crucial for plant health and water retention. Composting, mulch application, and natural soil amendments can be used to improve soil health, leading to stronger, more disease-resistant plants that require less water and chemical input.

Principle #3—Preserve Existing Plants

Preserving existing plants, particularly native species, can help maintain biodiversity, provide habitats for local wildlife, and reduce landscaping efforts. These plants are adapted to local climate conditions, pests, and diseases and typically require less maintenance and water than non-native species.

Principle #4—Conserve Material Resources

This principle focuses on reducing, reusing, and recycling materials in the landscape. It might mean repurposing existing on-site materials, using recycled or sustainably sourced products, composting garden waste, or opting for permeable paving to reduce stormwater runoff. These practices can reduce the environmental footprint of your landscape while promoting overall sustainability.

Key Components of Sustainable Landscaping

As discussed earlier, water conservation is a cornerstone of drought landscaping. From selecting drought-tolerant species to installing efficient irrigation systems, every decision made in landscape design should consider its water implications.

Use Native Plants to Reduce Pesticides

Native plants are naturally adapted to local conditions, making them more resistant to local pests and diseases. As a result, they require fewer chemical pesticides, reducing potential harm to beneficial insects, birds, and other local wildlife.

Use Trees to Provide Shade for Buildings and Reduce Energy Costs

Trees are true champions of our natural environment. They provide natural shade, reducing the need for air conditioning in warmer months and acting as windbreaks in cooler months. Moreover, their capacity to absorb carbon dioxide makes them crucial players in maintaining the balance of our atmosphere.

Use Ground Cover Plants to Reduce Erosion

Ground cover plants help prevent soil erosion, retain soil moisture, and suppress weeds. In addition to their functional benefits, they can add beautiful texture and color to your landscape.

Maximize Green Space Throughout All Seasons

Ensuring your landscape remains green and lush throughout the year not only improves its aesthetic appeal but also contributes to local biodiversity and ecosystem health. This can be achieved by choosing a variety of plants with different blooming seasons and using evergreen species.

Practical Ways to Incorporate Sustainability Into Landscape Design

The following steps outline practical strategies for incorporating these principles into your landscape design.

Learn About Your Landscape

A thorough understanding of your landscape, including its microclimates, soil types, and local conditions, is the first step in creating a sustainable landscape design. This knowledge forms the basis for informed decision-making throughout the design and implementation process.

Build Healthy Soil

Good soil health is the foundation for a thriving garden. Building healthy soil involves using organic matter like compost and mulch, avoiding soil compaction, and practicing proper watering techniques.

Choose the Right Plant

Selecting appropriate plants that are well suited for specific locations within your landscape is of paramount importance. Plants in suitable locations are healthier, require less maintenance, and create a more harmonious and visually pleasing landscape.

Reduce Waste and Recycle Nutrients

Composting garden waste is an excellent way to recycle nutrients and reduce the amount of waste sent to landfills. Compost improves soil structure, retains moisture, and provides a slow-release source of nutrients to plants.

Attract and Protect Wildlife

A diverse landscape attracts a variety of birds, insects, and other wildlife, contributing to a balanced ecosystem. Providing sources of food, water, and shelter can help support local wildlife populations.

Manage Yard Pests Responsibly

Managing pests responsibly involves a combination of practices, including fostering beneficial insects, using organic pesticides, and resorting to synthetic pesticides only as a last resort.

Mow and Prune Responsibly

Responsible mowing and pruning practices help maintain plant health and structure, reducing the need for supplemental water, fertilizers, and pesticides.

Reduce Stormwater Runoff

Reducing stormwater runoff can be accomplished through a combination of methods, which may involve incorporating permeable surfaces, establishing rain gardens or bioswales, and strategically planting trees and shrubs in appropriate locations.

Drought landscaping represents an excellent strategy for sustainability. The principles discussed provide a roadmap for creating landscapes that are both beautiful and sustainable, capable of enduring changing climatic conditions while supporting local biodiversity and ecosystem health. With a thoughtful and informed approach to our landscapes, we can each make a meaningful contribution to a more sustainable future.

Designing a drought-resistant and sustainable landscape is a multifaceted process that incorporates various elements. It's a careful amalgamation of water conservation strategies, understanding soil and climate conditions, plant selection, and aesthetics.

THE FOUNDATIONS OF LANDSCAPE DESIGN

Drawing a Scale Map

Start by drawing a detailed scale map of your property. This step ensures that you account for all aspects of your property before embarking on the actual design process. Your map should include clearly delineated property lines, a north arrow indicating the orientation, and a scale bar to indicate the proportional distance measurement used. It's also vital to note the contour of the land, as this can significantly influence the drainage and, subsequently, your landscape's ability to resist drought. Incorporate arrows on the map to visually represent the direction of surface-water flow.

Be sure to capture the locations of present landscaping elements, such as your residence, storage units, additional structures, greenery, trails, and parking areas on your plan. Also, consider the arrangement of entrances, windows, verandas, and interior spaces in your dwelling as these elements help shape the relationship between your house and the encompassing terrain. Identify and note down any views you appreciate or undesirable features on your property or adjoining properties. This will help you strategize and optimize the views and manage or disguise the less attractive aspects.

Completing a Site Analysis

Conducting a site analysis is crucial for understanding the existing conditions of your landscape. It helps you gain insights into soil type, existing vegetation, climate, and sun/shade exposure. Knowledge about these aspects enables you to select plants that thrive in your specific conditions, ensuring long-term sustainability and drought resistance.

Assessing Family Needs

Take time to evaluate how you and your family plan to use the landscape. This helps to determine the different use areas required, which could include public areas for socializing, private or family areas that ensure privacy and comfort, children's play areas, or service and work areas for practical tasks like gardening or washing cars. All these areas have unique requirements and will influence the final design of your landscape.

Structuring Your Landscape: Determining Use Areas

When it comes to planning your landscape, one principle to keep in mind is the division of space according to different needs. Understanding your family's requirements and lifestyle habits will help guide this process.

The Public Area

Typically, the front yard serves as the prominent and welcoming face of your property. It's often more formal and aims to add curb appeal and enhance the overall aesthetic of your home from the street. The design should be inviting, with thoughtfully placed plants that are drought-resistant and hardy, reducing maintenance needs.

The Private or Family Area

These spaces are typically the backyard or side yards, meant for relaxation, entertainment, and other private family activities.

They can be designed for privacy, year-round interest, and climate control. The plant selection here should focus on providing shade, possibly reducing home cooling costs, and creating attractive views from inside the home. Drought-resistant plants are especially important in these areas, as they often get more use and, therefore, more wear and tear.

Children's Play Area

If you have children, a dedicated play area can be a wonderful addition to your landscape. This area should be safe, engaging, and resilient to heavy use. Durable, low-maintenance, and non-toxic plants are ideal for these spaces.

Service and Work Areas

These are utilitarian areas used for tasks such as composting, gardening, or storing tools. Even though these are functional spaces, they should be designed to blend seamlessly with the rest of the landscape, using appropriate plants and materials that are drought resistant and low maintenance.

Creating a Landscape That Lasts: Evaluating Sustainability

As you go through the process of designing your landscape, it's crucial to consider its sustainability. A sustainable landscape is characterized by its alignment with the local climate and its ability to operate with minimal resource inputs, including water, fertilizer, and labor. It's not only beneficial for the environment but also requires less maintenance and expense over time.

To achieve a sustainable landscape, you should choose native or locally adapted plants, which are typically more drought resistant and pest resistant. Incorporate water-conserving practices, like rainwater harvesting and efficient irrigation systems. Use composting and mulching to improve soil health and reduce the need for synthetic fertilizers.

Infusing Creativity

Maintain simplicity in design. This does not mean your landscape design has to be boring, but rather that it should avoid unnecessary complexity. A design that is easy to understand and navigate creates a sense of peace and harmony.

Rhythm and Line

The lines and shapes you use in your design can guide the eye and movement through the landscape. Curving lines can create a relaxed, natural feel, while straight lines often lend a more formal, orderly look.

Balance

Balance is crucial in landscape design. It can be either symmetrical, where elements on both sides of the landscape are mirror images of each other, or asymmetrical, where different elements balance each other out in size, form, or color.

Proportion

Ensure that all elements, including plants, hardscape elements, and features, are in proportion to each other and to the overall landscape. Large features or plants can overwhelm a small space, while small elements can be lost in a large area.

Focal Point

Every good design should have one or more focal points. This could be a tree, a statue, a water feature, or a colorful plant. The focal point draws the eye and provides a place for it to rest, adding interest and depth to your landscape.

Once you have brainstormed and planned, it's time to create a scaled drawing of your design. This detailed plan should include all elements you intend to incorporate into your landscape, including plants, hardscapes, and features.

Designing a drought-resistant and sustainable landscape can be a rewarding process. It's about understanding your property's unique characteristics, respecting the local environment, and creating a beautiful, functional space for you and your family to enjoy. With thoughtful planning and design, your landscape can be a source of joy, a haven for local wildlife, and a testament to sustainable practices.

Remember, your landscape will grow and evolve over time, so be patient and enjoy the journey. Keep refining and tweaking, and most importantly, keep learning. After all, every gardener is a lifelong student of nature.

THE 3 PS OF DROUGHT LANDSCAPING: PREPARE, PLANT, PRESERVE

In this chapter, we have delved deep into the myriad aspects of designing a drought-resistant and sustainable landscape. From selecting drought-tolerant plants and amending soil quality to planning garden beds and mastering resourceful irrigation, there's a lot to digest. These tasks might seem overwhelming, but there's a way to streamline this process. This approach is encapsulated in what we call the "3 Ps of drought landscaping." Prepare, Plant, and Preserve. These simple yet powerful concepts will guide you through creating a sustainable and resilient outdoor space.

Prepare: Setting the Foundation for Success

The first "P," prepare, starts with selecting the right plants for your garden. Drought-resistant plants, particularly native species, are the cornerstone of any drought-tolerant landscape. These hardy plants have evolved to thrive in your local climate and soil conditions, making them ideal for a low-maintenance, water-wise garden.

Native plants provide a habitat for local wildlife, add natural beauty to your landscape, and increase its resilience. They also contribute to the overall sustainability of your landscape, as they typically require fewer resources and less care than non-native species. Research local native plant species and consider their needs and characteristics. What are their water, light, and soil requirements? How large will they grow? What are their bloom times and colors? These factors will influence your overall landscape design.

Understanding and Improving Soil Quality

Healthy, well-amended soil is crucial for plant health and drought resistance. Soil acts as a reservoir for water and nutrients, and its condition can significantly impact the health of your plants and their ability to withstand drought.

Start by analyzing your soil. Is it sandy and well-draining, or is it heavy clay that retains water? Every soil type comes with its own set of advantages and challenges. Familiarizing yourself with your soil will assist you in choosing plants that will flourish and provide guidance on amending the soil if needed.

Enhancing soil quality frequently entails incorporating organic matter, such as compost, to augment its capacity for retaining water and to enhance its nutrient content. Properly prepared soil will help your plants establish more quickly and resist drought better.

Plant

The second "P," plant, involves considering the layout of your garden beds. Thoughtful placement and design of garden beds can significantly reduce water runoff, helping to conserve water and prevent soil erosion.

Consider the slope of your land. Beds designed along contour lines can help capture rainwater and allow it to infiltrate the soil. Raised beds can help improve drainage, while recessed beds, or rain gardens, can help capture and filter runoff.

Practicing Mulching

Mulching is another key element in your planning process. Applying a layer of mulch to the soil surface aids in preserving moisture, suppressing weed growth, and promoting a consistent soil temperature. Organic mulches, such as compost, wood chips, or straw, can also improve your soil's health over time as they break down. Plan to incorporate mulching into your garden beds and around your plants.

Preserve: Maintaining Your Landscape Sustainably

The third "P," preserve, entails the ongoing care and maintenance of your landscape. Key to this is the use of sustainable
watering and irrigation methods.

Watering deeply and infrequently encourages plants to develop
deep roots, enhancing their drought tolerance. Early-morning
watering reduces water loss to evaporation. Drip irrigation
systems are highly efficient in providing water directly to the
root zone of plants, resulting in minimal water wastage and
facilitating optimal hydration for plants.

Rainwater Harvesting

Consider integrating rainwater harvesting into your landscape.
Rain barrels or more complex cistern systems can capture valuable rainwater runoff from your roof, which can then be used
to water your plants. Not only does this conserve water, but
rainwater is also beneficial for your plants, as it is naturally soft
and free of chlorine and other chemicals found in municipal
water supplies.

Pest Management and General Maintenance

Finally, sustainable pest management is an important aspect of
preserving your landscape. Many native plants are naturally
resistant to local pests, but healthy soil and regular maintenance are also key to preventing pest issues.

Adopting a proactive approach, such as regularly checking
plants for signs of stress or disease, can help catch and mitigate

issues early. When necessary, opt for organic or environmentally friendly pest solutions.

Remember, your landscape is a living, dynamic system. Regular maintenance, from pruning to weeding, will help keep it looking its best and functioning smoothly.

In essence, by adhering to these 3 Ps—prepare, plant, and preserve—you can create a resilient, water-wise, and beautiful landscape. Not only will you contribute positively to your local ecosystem, but you'll also have a unique outdoor space to enjoy and be proud of. No matter how daunting the process may seem at first, remember that each small step brings you closer to your sustainable landscaping goal.

INTERACTIVE ELEMENT: QUESTIONNAIRE FOR LANDSCAPE DESIGN PLANNING

Section 1: Gathering Site Information

- What is the color of your house?
- What is the architectural style of your house?
- What views from your property do you find appealing?
- What views would you rather hide or divert attention from?
- Are there any overhead utilities?
- What unique features does your landscape currently possess?
- What is the usual direction of winds during summer and winter?

- Do you require wind screens? If yes, where would you place them?
- Do you require sound buffers? If yes, where would you need them?
- Do you have any elevation differences in your yard: minimal, moderate, or severe slopes?
- Do you need retaining walls? If yes, where would you position them?
- Do you have any areas with a high water table?
- Where does water typically find its way out?
- Is there a need for a French drain?
- How would you characterize the amount of sunlight your yard receives?
- Which areas of your yard tend to overheat during summer?
- What trees, shrubs, or exposed roots are already present in your yard?
- What existing features and structures are found on your property?
- What is the nature of the pathways in your yard: brick, concrete, gravel, stone, or bark?
- Do you own a parking strip? If so, where can it be found?
- How often do you plan on maintaining your yard: often, regularly, or rarely?

Section 2: Design Considerations

- Who are the primary users of your yard: adults, kids, older individuals, or pets?

- What's your desired aesthetic: formal, semiformal, casual, or theme-based (such as English, Asian, or natural)?
- What shape appeals to you for lawns, paths, and decks: square, 45° angles, circles, straight lines, wavy/free-form, or a mixture?
- What kind of front entranceway do you favor: direct route to the door, winding path, or private courtyard?

Answering these questions will give you a solid understanding of your current landscape and provide valuable input as you plan your new design. Remember, the more detailed your answers, the more precise your landscape planning can be!

CONCLUSION

Designing a drought-resistant and sustainable landscape is an exciting journey that not only makes your yard more environmentally friendly but also significantly reduces your maintenance efforts and costs. By meticulously preparing, planning, and preserving, you can transform your landscape into a sustainable oasis that thrives in drought conditions. Moreover, your selections of native and drought-tolerant plants, improved soil quality, strategically planned garden beds, and resourceful irrigation practices will contribute significantly to overcoming water runoff and conservation challenges.

Remember to use the interactive questionnaire to understand your unique needs and preferences better, which in turn will greatly aid your planning process. With all these tools and principles at your disposal, you are well-equipped to create a landscape that is both beautiful and resilient.

3

NATURE FINDS A WAY

We all remember as children, when we were awestruck by the wonders of nature, how our sense of marvel reached new heights. Perhaps it was the discovery of a green shoot stubbornly poking its way through the cracks of a city sidewalk or the sudden bloom of wildflowers in a barren field. Unyielding, resilient, ever hopeful—these are the qualities that make up the fabric of nature. As we embark on the journey to explore sustainable landscaping in this chapter, we shall keep this steadfast spirit of nature as our guiding star.

"To me more dear, congenial to my heart, One native charm, than all the gloss of art" (Goldsmith, 2008). With these soulful words from Oliver Goldsmith, we journey toward one of the "Ps" of our 3-P approach—plants. But not just any plants. We turn our attention to the unsung heroes of the plant kingdom: the native plants.

Why native plants? For starters, they have been here long before we staked our claim on the land. They have weathered the winds of change, faced the harsh glare of the sun, and drawn sustenance from the depths of the earth. They are the original inhabitants, harmoniously coexisting with local fauna, enriching the soil, and fostering biodiversity. They are the embodiment of resilience and adaptability—exactly what we need as we strive toward drought-resistant landscapes.

This chapter will serve as your guide to understanding native plants and their remarkable benefits. We will explore why they are an excellent choice when planning sustainable, low-mainte-nance, and beautiful landscapes. Moreover, you will discover how native plants contribute to creating healthier living spaces, conserving water, and supporting local wildlife.

Drawing from reliable sources such as *The Nature of Cities* and *Audubon*, we will examine the advantages of these local botanical heroes and delve into their unique characteristics that make them so advantageous. You will discover that they require less water and fertilizer, are seldom invasive, and thrive with less intensive labor than many other commonly used plants. They are loved by pollinators, support local communities, and play a vital role in preserving biodiversity and at-risk species.

From the vast range of native plant types (flowering plants, grasses, groundcovers, trees, and shrubs) you will learn how to identify and choose those most suitable for your yard. This chapter will also help you navigate through the world of native cultivars and understand their role in your yard.

As we unfold the secrets of landscaping with native plants, we will also touch upon vital topics like topography and hydrology, woodland succession, and dealing with invasive exotic species. We will go on a virtual tour of naturalistic landscapes and help you understand how they can be translated into a vibrant, beautiful, and ecologically sound garden.

In addition, we will provide tips on how to maximize the potential of your native plant garden, how to select drought-tolerant plants, and how to introduce native grasses into your landscape. All these elements will combine to create a stunning landscape that will be a joy for you and a haven for local wildlife.

To ensure you have a practical approach in hand, we will guide you through a landscape-design planning questionnaire that brings together all the essential points discussed in this chapter. In addition, the appendix and resources provided will give you further insights into creating your perfect garden.

So, buckle up and get ready to embark on a journey that takes you back to your roots, quite literally. Let's open our hearts and our gardens to the native charms that lie waiting to be rediscovered as we remind ourselves that, indeed, Nature always finds a way.

ACTIVELY NATIVE: THE ADVANTAGES OF NATIVE PLANTS

The planting of native plants has become a popular trend in modern landscaping. This isn't merely a passing fad; it's a step toward preserving and restoring our ecosystems. Indigenous flora, which originates and naturally adapts within a specific region, acts as the ecological foundation that sustains a diverse range of life forms. Their significance goes beyond aesthetics, offering a myriad of environmental benefits, from water conservation to boosting biodiversity.

Why They Matter

Over the last century, human activities have fragmented and transformed ecologically productive land into urban areas, leaving wildlife struggling to survive. The concerning transformation, driven by uncontrolled urban expansion and a fixation with impeccably maintained lawns, has led to the startling disappearance of 150 million acres of habitats and agricultural lands in the US. Areas now under extensive human influence have lost their ability to maintain operational ecosystems, and the sparse remaining patches of untouched nature are inadequate to sustain wildlife.

Native plants, adapted to thrive in their specific environment, act as the life support for local birds, insects, and other organisms that have coevolved alongside them. A stark example is the native oak tree, which supports over 500 species of caterpillars. In contrast, an exotic ginkgo tree hosts a mere five. The implications for the bird population are substantial when considering that approximately 6,000 caterpillars are required to nurture a single brood of chickadees.

Unfortunately, the bulk of plants found in gardening stores are foreign species brought in from overseas. These non-native plants have the potential to upset the balance of the food chain, often evolving into invasive species that overpower local plants and further degrade the condition of the few remaining natural habitats. Hence, the decisions we make about our landscaping can have a profound effect on the survival of bird species and the insects they rely on for sustenance.

The Environmental Payoff

When comparing native plants to non-native ones, it becomes evident that native plants necessitate less maintenance. They have evolved to flourish in their local environment, enduring their weather patterns, pests, and soil conditions. As a result, they generally need less water, reducing the necessity for frequent irrigation and saving a valuable natural resource. Their adaptability also means they require less fertilizer, if any, as they can thrive off the nutrients available in their ecosystem's soil. This cuts back on time, money, and environmental impact since synthetic fertilizers can lead to toxic stormwater runoff, affecting aquatic organisms.

Healthy Spaces for People

Native plants promote healthier spaces for people. Traditional lawns are notorious for their dependence on synthetic chemical pesticides and artificial fertilizers. By contrast, native plants have natural defenses against local pests, negating the need for harmful pesticides. With native plants, your garden becomes a healthier place for you and your community, free from the harmful toxins present in many chemical pesticides and fertilizers.

Beauty and Biodiversity

Native plants captivate with their diverse array of shapes, hues, and sizes. The radiant blooms, vibrant fruits and seeds, along with the dynamic seasonal color shifts, bring unique beauty to your garden while promoting biodiversity. Each garden cultivated with local flora contributes to a shared endeavor to protect and nurture the rich diversity of life within the landscape, encouraging the interdependence of numerous organisms.

Encouraging Wildlife

Native plants play a significant role in sustaining wildlife. They provide shelter, nectar for pollinators, and essential foods like nuts, seeds, and fruits for various forms of wildlife. A landscape rich in native plants attracts an array of beautiful butterflies, hummingbirds, and bees, and even provides an essential habitat for bats and mammals.

Moreover, native plants are seldom invasive, unlike many non-native plants that can dominate an area and upset the ecological balance. Native plants contribute to maintaining equilibrium in your garden while also promoting biodiversity.

GETTING THE MOST OUT OF YOUR NATIVE PLANT GARDEN

Choosing native plants for your garden or landscape can be a rewarding endeavor. However, acquiring knowledge about the native plant species in your specific area, as well as the types of birds and other wildlife they can attract, is essential.

Utilize local resources, join native plant societies, and tap into databases such as *Audubon's* to discover native plants in your area.

Native plant gardening can be transformative, not just for your yard but for your local ecosystem. It's an act that supports biodiversity and benefits the community while also creating a beautiful, low-maintenance, and healthy space for you to enjoy. It's time to go native!

Going native isn't just about gardening; it's about being a responsible steward of the land. It's about making conscious decisions that respect and support our environment. Native plants aren't just a landscaping trend; they're a powerful tool for creating sustainable, diverse, and resilient ecosystems. So, let's embrace the beauty and benefits of native plants for our gardens, our communities, and our planet.

Native Plant Types

Understanding native plants and their roles in creating a sustainable environment isn't just for the green-thumbed enthusiasts. The way we landscape and cultivate our outdoor spaces impacts the natural biodiversity, the health of local ecosystems, and, ultimately, the sustainability of our planet. So, let's dig deeper and explore various native plant types, their uses, and some helpful tips on integrating them into your surroundings.

Non-Woody Flowering Plants

Non-woody flowering plants encompass a vast array of species, each with unique characteristics, adaptability to various climates, and ecological benefits. One prominent category within this group is berries.

Serviceberries (*Amelanchier* spp.)

They not only enhance the beauty of the landscape with their white spring flowers and vibrant fall foliage but also play a crucial role in supporting caterpillars and attracting butterflies. Furthermore, they produce berries that serve as a delightful feast for birds and also possess a pleasing taste for human palates.

Elderberries (*Sambucus* spp.)

Elderberries, either as trees or small shrubs, offer more than just aesthetics. They grow between 5 and 12 ft tall and serve as the primary food source for various caterpillars, including those of the cecropia moth. In addition to their aesthetic value, they play a vital role in supporting the life cycle of these caterpillars. The dark purple berries, believed to be rich in Vitamin C, fiber, and antioxidants, may have health benefits for humans, though they are also loved by birds.

Blueberries and Sparkleberries (*Vaccinium* spp.)

They can be consumed by humans and encompass well-known fruits such as cranberries, huckleberries, and lingonberries. They originate from regions within the US, with Maine standing as the globe's leading producer of wild blueberries.

Grasses and Groundcovers

Grasses and groundcovers, including vines, provide a diverse range of textures, colors, and functions. They prevent soil erosion, regulate soil temperature, and enhance the overall aesthetic appeal of your landscape.

The honeysuckles (*Lonicera* spp.) are a great choice. Easy to grow and demanding little care, with their vibrant springtime blossoms and the allure of their fall berries, these native plants have the ability to infuse any garden or street with a delightful splash of color. However, it's crucial to choose a native species to prevent ecological harm.

Among grasses, switchgrass (*Panicum* spp.) and muhly grass (*Muhlenbergia* spp.) are popular choices. Switchgrass, a native species to the eastern regions of the United States, boasts over 400 different varieties. Flourishing under abundant sunlight, this resilient plant requires minimal maintenance for healthy growth. Muhly grass, hardy and drought-resistant, displays fluffy plumes of color, becoming a buffet for many songbirds when the seeds take over in November.

Trees and Shrubs

Native trees and shrubs are vital for landscaping, providing not only aesthetic beauty but also essential habitats and food for local wildlife.

We already touched on some berry-producing trees like the serviceberry and elderberry. However, it's crucial to note that when choosing native trees and shrubs for landscaping, factors such as the plant's size, its compatibility with your region's climate, soil type, and the amount of sunlight it requires should be considered.

LANDSCAPING WITH THE NATIVES

While native plants can beautify your surroundings, under-standing the principles of landscaping with them can help you create a healthy and sustainable ecosystem in your backyard.

Topography and Hydrology

Understanding the topography and hydrology of your area is crucial when planning a native garden. Over thousands of years, native plants have undergone a process of adaptation to suit the local conditions of their respective regions. This extensive period of evolution has allowed them to thrive and effectively cope with the specific environmental factors in their native habitats, and selecting species suitable for your specific environment will increase their survival rate and minimize the need for intensive care.

Woodland Succession

Understanding the concept of woodland succession can help to establish a successful native garden. In essence, it is the ecological process that follows a disturbance in an area. Over time, one group of plants and animals replaces another, contributing to a more diverse ecosystem.

Physiographic Regions and Forest-Community Types

Knowing your physiographic region and forest-community type can guide you in choosing the right native plants. It can help you recreate a natural habitat that will attract local wildlife and contribute to the overall health of your ecosystem.

Invasive Exotic Species Management

Invasive exotic species can harm local ecosystems, outcompeting native species for resources. Therefore, it's important to manage and remove these species and replace them with natives.

Aesthetic Concerns of Naturalistic Landscapes

While naturalistic landscapes offer numerous environmental benefits, aesthetics should not be overlooked. Consider the color, texture, and form of the plants you choose to create an appealing visual tableau that changes with the seasons.

HOW TO FIND NATIVE PLANTS FOR YOUR YARD

Finding native plants for your yard can be as simple as visiting a local nursery specializing in native plants or searching online databases and plant finder tools that allow you to input your zip code to find plants suited to your region.

Tips on How to Use Native Plants

Gardens Galore

Native plants can be used to create various types of gardens, from butterfly gardens to rain gardens. The choices are endless, and each offers a unique set of benefits.

Time the Blossoms

Consider choosing plants that bloom at different times of the year to ensure a continual food supply for pollinators and continuous aesthetic appeal.

Get Creative in Winter

Choose native plants that provide winter interest with colorful bark, interesting silhouettes, or evergreen foliage.

Replace Your Turfgrass

Consider replacing traditional lawn grasses with native ground covers, which require less water and care and provide a better habitat for local wildlife.

Hire a Professional Eye

If you're not sure where to start, consider hiring a landscape architect or designer familiar with native plants. Their knowledge and experience can save you time and money in the long run.

Native Cultivars vs. Straight Species Native Plants

Native cultivars are a type of native plant that has been selectively bred for certain characteristics, such as color or disease resistance. In contrast, straight-species native plants, also known as "indigenous plants," are those that have not been genetically altered.

Are Native Cultivars the Right Plants for You?

This depends on several factors, such as your specific aesthetic preferences and environmental conditions. Both native cultivars and straight species have pros and cons, and some may be more suited to your needs than others.

How to Differentiate Between Natives and Other Cultivars

Differentiating between natives and other cultivars requires research. Check with a trusted nursery, use online databases, or hire a professional to help you select the best native plants for your needs. Ultimately, the native plants you choose should support local ecosystems, contribute to biodiversity, and bring you joy.

Checklist for Selecting Drought-Tolerant Plants

Selecting drought-tolerant plants is a crucial aspect of sustainable landscaping, particularly in regions prone to water scarcity. Below is a checklist of considerations to guide you when choosing plants for a drought-resistant landscape.

Aesthetic Considerations

First and foremost, consider the aesthetic appeal of the plants. While it's essential to select drought-tolerant species, they should also contribute to the visual beauty of your landscape. This involves examining their color, bloom period, and contribution to the overall design of your garden.

Mature Size

It is important to consider the mature size of the plants in question. By following this approach, you can ensure that your selected plants have sufficient space to grow, preventing overcrowding or hindrance to each other's growth. Understanding the full growth potential of a plant will help you determine its placement in the landscape, maximizing its aesthetic and functional benefits.

Plant Form

The form of the plant—whether it's a tree, shrub, or ground cover—will also influence your selection. Different forms serve different functions, such as providing shade, controlling erosion, or simply adding color. Your choice should align with your overall landscape design and specific needs.

Plant Texture

Plant texture can dramatically influence your landscape's appearance. Fine-textured plants can create a sense of distance, while coarse-textured plants tend to draw attention and seem closer. Mixing textures can add contrast and visual interest to your garden.

Design Considerations

Design considerations are paramount. The height, width, shape, and color of plants should all be chosen with your design goals in mind. Consider whether you need plants to conserve energy, control erosion, or attract local fauna, such as birds and butterflies.

Choose Adapted Plants

Your selected plants should be well suited to your local environment. This includes compatibility with your region's soil, water availability, temperature ranges, and light levels. In many cases, this doesn't limit you to native plants only, as many species from around the world may be well adapted to your local conditions.

Hydrozones

Organize your plants according to their water needs. This method, known as creating hydrozones, leads to efficient watering practices as it reduces the risk of overwatering or underwatering your plants.

Seasonal Interest

Choose plants that provide visual interest throughout the year. By selecting plants with varying bloom times and seasonal features, you can ensure your garden remains vibrant and appealing year-round.

Hardiness Zone

Check the USDA Plant Hardiness Zone Map to determine which plants are most likely to thrive in your area's climate (USDA, 2020). Take into account the minimum annual survival temperatures for each plant, and ensure they align with your region's typical conditions.

Native Grasses and Non-Native Plants

Consider incorporating native grasses into your landscape, as they're generally well adapted to local climates and require less maintenance and water. On the flip side, certain non-native plants should be avoided or removed due to their potential to become invasive or their inability to thrive without excessive care and water.

Creating a drought-resistant landscape involves more than just picking plants that can survive with less water. It's about finding a balance between sustainability, functionality, and aesthetics, taking into consideration a range of factors from soil type to hardiness zones. By adhering to this checklist, you'll be on the right path toward creating a beautiful, resilient, and water-wise garden.

LANDSCAPE DESIGN PLANNING QUESTIONNAIRE: PLANTS

Let's delve into the most vibrant and life-giving aspect of your landscape—the plants. Here, we will consider your preferences, the potential benefits of native plants, and the significance of drought-resistant selections.

Flora Preferences

- What are your plant preferences?
- For evergreen trees and shrubs, do you prefer those that flower or those that don't?
- Where would you like the placement of the deciduous trees and shrubs?
- What are your thoughts on coniferous trees, fruit-bearing trees, trees that provide shade, junipers, climbing plants, or roses?
- Would you be interested in annual or perennial flowers, vegetables, or herbs?

Consider adding some local or drought-resistant plants to your collection. These plants usually need less upkeep and watering than non-native varieties. They also enhance biodiversity and offer a habitat for regional wildlife.

Sensory Preferences

- Do you appreciate plants with a fragrance? Yes or no.
- What are your color preferences?

The color scheme of your garden can significantly affect its ambience and visual allure. Bear in mind that native and drought-resistant plants might not match your color preferences perfectly. However, their ecological benefits often supersede color concerns.

Lawn Specifications

- How much expansion do you envisage for your lawn? Choose between none, small, average, or large.
- What is your preferred location for the placement of the lawn?

It's essential to note that maintaining a lawn can consume a substantial amount of water. If you opt for a larger lawn, we suggest using drought-resistant grass types or replacing some lawn sections with similar ground covers.

Allergies and Interactions With Wildlife

- Does anyone in your household suffer from allergies to particular plants or bees? Yes or no.
- Are you experiencing issues with deer?

It's worth noting that numerous native plants can attract pollinators like bees. If allergies are a concern, you can choose
plants that are less attractive to bees. For deer problems, you
can select plants that are naturally resistant to these animals.

Distinctive Garden Spaces

- Do you have any particular areas in your garden in
  mind?

Options could include vegetable patches, annual flower beds,
rose gardens, perennial areas, herb gardens, wildlife/native
plant areas, orchards, shade spots, rock gardens, cut-flower
gardens, fragrance gardens, wheelchair-accessible areas, or any
other specific spaces.

CONCLUSION

In this chapter, we journeyed into the enchanting realm of
native and drought-resistant plants, discovering their essential
role in sustainable and water-efficient landscape design.
Drawing on the second "P" of our 3-P approach, plants, we
explored the multifaceted benefits native plants bring to our
gardens, from low-maintenance requirements to fostering
biodiversity and preserving our climate to conserving precious
water resources. We delved into the types of native plants,
offering practical guidance on how to incorporate them seamlessly into your landscape. Equally important, we embarked on
introducing a practical guide for selecting drought-tolerant

plants and offered key considerations to bear in mind during this process. Armed with these insights, you're now well equipped to craft a garden that not only radiates beauty but also champions sustainability.

4

HOME IS WHERE THE ROOTS ARE

There's a potent wisdom that exists beneath our feet, unseen yet profoundly influential—it is the wisdom of the soil. Franklin D. Roosevelt, America's 32nd president, astutely observed, "The Nation that destroys its soil destroys itself." This chapter, dear reader, is an invitation to a deeper understanding of this wisdom, an invitation to engage with the soil, the silent yet profound foundation of all life on our planet.

Soil isn't just a medium for planting; it is the essence that nurtures life, enabling the magnificence of gardens to spring forth and thrive. Each handful of soil is a universe in itself, teeming with countless micro-organisms that sustain and enhance life above the ground. As gardeners and landscape enthusiasts, our success largely depends on understanding this subterranean universe. Yet, how much do we genuinely know about our soil? How often do we stop and consider its unique characteristics or even acknowledge its existence in our gardening journey?

This chapter aims to enhance your soil literacy, offering insight into the soil's types and characteristics, their importance in gardening and landscaping, and how to assess and work with them. We'll journey into the depths of clay and sandy soils and traverse the richness of silt, loam, peat, and chalky soils, each with its distinctive traits and nurturing capacities.

Together, we'll explore the often-overlooked practice of soil testing—a gardener's secret tool for thriving landscapes. This will be more than just an academic exercise. It's an invitation to engage with your garden at a deeper level, to truly see your soil, to appreciate its complexity and diversity. By understanding its nature, nutritional composition, and pH levels, you'll be better equipped to meet your garden's needs, making you an eco-friendly gardener who saves time and money and contributes to a healthier ecosystem.

Prepare to roll up your sleeves as we dive into practical, hands-on methods of soil testing. We'll guide you through simple DIY tests you can conduct in your own backyard using everyday materials. This is about empowering you to read your soil, interpret its story, and work in harmony with it to create landscapes that are vibrant, sustainable, and resilient.

So, let's embark on this journey of discovery and connection. After all, our gardens are as healthy as the soil they grow in, and understanding our soil is the first step toward becoming custodians of the land rather than mere consumers.

Welcome to Chapter 4, "Home Is Where the Roots Are," where we'll delve into the marvelous world of soil and the powerful, intimate role it plays in our lives as gardeners. It's time to get our hands dirty and our hearts full.

UNDERSTANDING SOIL: TYPES AND CHARACTERISTICS

The earth beneath our feet is not simply dirt. It's a vibrant ecosystem teeming with life and brimming with complexities that make it an essential part of our environment. This complex system is soil. From supporting plant growth to playing a significant role in the earth's water cycle and serving as a habitat for countless organisms, the soil is an indispensable part of our biosphere.

What Is Soil?

Soil refers to a naturally existing blend of mineral and organic components that possess a distinct shape, arrangement, and makeup. It's the upper layer of the earth where plants have their roots, and it's made up of numerous components, including decayed plant and animal material, organic matter, micro-organisms, minerals, and weathered rock. Soil forms over many years and is responsible for sustaining most of Earth's terrestrial life.

The diverse nature of soil gives it the ability to fulfill various roles in our environment. It serves as the medium for plant growth, acting as an anchor for plant roots and providing essential nutrients. Soil also plays a vital role in water regulation, absorbing rain and snow and slowly releasing it over time. It's an essential participant in biogeochemical cycles, facilitating the transfer of substances like carbon and nitrogen between living and nonliving parts of the ecosystem.

In addition, the soil is a habitat for an enormous variety of organisms, from tiny bacteria to larger creatures like insects and earthworms, each playing a crucial role in the soil ecosystem. Beyond its ecological functions, soil also serves practical purposes, such as providing the base for infrastructure and the raw material for industries like ceramics.

Now, let's dive deeper into the types of soil and their characteristics to understand this complex system better.

Types of Soils and Their Characteristics

Though soil is found everywhere, it's not the same everywhere you go. Several soil types exist, each with unique characteristics. Below, we explore some of the most common types: sand, clay, silt, loam, chalk, and peat.

Sand

Sandy soil is primarily composed of tiny rock and mineral particles, which gives it a coarse texture. Being light, dry, and warm, this soil type tends to drain quickly and has a low water-retention capacity, making it prone to drying out. Despite its challenges for plant growth, due to the lack of moisture and nutrients, sandy soil can be improved by adding organic matter, which enhances its water and nutrient content, making it more conducive for cultivation.

Clay

Clay soil has a distinct, heavy feel due to its high water-retention capacity and nutrient content. It's composed of over 25% clay particles, which are smaller in size, allowing the soil to hold large amounts of water. This soil type drains slowly and takes longer to warm up during the summer. Its density can make it challenging for plant roots to flourish. However, with careful management, clay soil can be highly productive, as it's rich in nutrients that plants need.

Silt

Silt soil is light and has a smooth, fine quality due to its particle size, which is larger than clay but smaller than sand. This soil type is excellent at holding water, making it more fertile than sandy soil. Its capacity to retain water and its relative fertility make silt soil a preferred choice for various agricultural practices. However, being easily transported by moving currents, it's commonly found near water bodies and can be susceptible to erosion if not managed properly.

Loam

Loam soil is often considered the gold standard for many gardeners and farmers as it perfectly combines the beneficial qualities of sand, silt, and clay soils. It has a well-balanced mixture of these three components, resulting in a soil type that has a good structure, ample pore space, and excellent water-retention capabilities. The presence of inorganic matter gives loam soil the right level of calcium and pH necessary for plant growth. This makes it highly fertile and ideal for growing a wide range of plants.

Chalk

Chalky soils are alkaline in nature due to the presence of limestone or chalk in their composition. These soils are typically stony and can drain quickly. Although chalky soils are often nutrient poor and can be challenging for certain plants that require more acidic or neutral pH levels, they can support a unique array of plant species adapted to these conditions.

Peat

Peat soils are unique due to their high organic-matter content. Formed from the partial decomposition of plant material in wet conditions, peat soil is dark, rich, and holds water exceptionally well. However, it doesn't naturally contain many nutrients that plants need to grow. Despite this, peat soil can be incredibly beneficial for plant growth when properly managed and amended with the necessary nutrients.

Understanding the characteristics of these different soil types is crucial for successful gardening and farming, as well as for making informed decisions about land management and conservation. Each soil type has its strengths and weaknesses, but with knowledge and careful management, each can play a significant role in supporting the diversity and productivity of our planet's ecosystems.

Working With Your Soil

Just as a chef understands the ingredients in their kitchen or an artist knows their paints, gardeners and farmers must comprehend the nature of their soil. Knowing your soil is the first step toward creating a thriving garden or productive farmland. Recognizing the characteristics of various soil types and how to work with them can help you avoid common problems and maximize your soil's potential.

Nurturing Sandy Soils

Sandy soils, characterized by their coarse texture and fast-draining nature, often struggle with nutrient and moisture retention. This quick drainage can lead to a soil environment that dries out quickly and lacks the necessary nutrients for optimal plant growth.

Improving sandy soil involves enhancing its ability to retain moisture and nutrients. This can be achieved by adding organic matter such as well-rotted manure or compost. These additions enrich the soil, increase its water-holding capacity, and slow down the leaching of nutrients. Mulching around plants can also assist in conserving moisture.

Working With Clay Soils

Clay soils are rich in nutrients and can retain water exceptionally well due to their dense structure and small particle size. However, they can present challenges due to their heavy nature and slow drainage, which can inhibit root growth and cause waterlogging in wet conditions.

To enhance clay soil, it is advisable to incorporate organic materials such as compost, manure, or leaf mold. The addition of organic matter aids in enhancing the structure of the soil by increasing its porosity, thereby facilitating root penetration. It also enhances the soil's drainage, reducing water logging while also helping it retain just the right amount of moisture.

Rotating your crops can also help prevent soil compaction, a common issue with clay soils. Deep-rooted plants, for example, can break up the soil and improve its structure. Remember to give clay soil time to dry out before working on it, as it can easily compact when wet.

Making the Most of Silt Soils

Silt soils, with their smooth, fine particles, have great fertility and water-retaining characteristics. They are generally considered ideal for most plants. However, they can compact easily and are prone to erosion.

To prevent soil compaction, it is important to avoid excessive watering and unnecessary foot traffic on the soil. Additionally, the inclusion of organic matter can be beneficial in enhancing the soil's structure and increasing its ability to resist erosion. Consider using cover crops and practicing crop rotation to keep your silt soil healthy and productive.

Leveraging Loams

Loam soils, with their well-balanced mix of sand, silt, and clay, are often considered ideal for gardening and farming. These soils have a good structure, drain well yet retain moisture, and are rich in nutrients.

Although loam soils are typically easier to manage, they can still benefit from the addition of organic matter to maintain their fertility and structure. Regular crop rotation and careful watering will keep your loam soil in top condition.

Coping with Chalky Soils

Chalky soils are alkaline due to the presence of limestone or chalk. They can be nutrient poor and dry out quickly due to fast drainage. These soils also contain calcium carbonate, which can make certain nutrients unavailable to plants.

To improve chalky soil, try adding organic matter, which can help retain moisture and improve nutrient content. Planting with species that thrive in alkaline conditions can also lead to successful cultivation.

Addressing Common Soil Problems

Even with a deep understanding of your soil type, you may still encounter issues. Here are some common soil problems and suggestions on how to deal with them:

- **poor drainage:** This issue often occurs in heavy clay soils. Improving drainage can be achieved by adding organic matter and creating raised beds to promote water runoff.
- **low fertility:** Sandy soils often suffer from this issue. Enhancing fertility can be done by regularly adding organic matter and using a slow-release fertilizer.

- **soil erosion:** This can be an issue for silt soils. Planting cover crops and adding organic matter can help bind the soil together and prevent erosion.
- **soil alkalinity:** Chalky soils tend to have this problem. Regularly adding organic matter can help lower the pH slightly. However, the most effective solution is often to plant species that thrive in alkaline conditions.

Understanding your soil and working with its natural strengths and weaknesses is key to successful gardening and farming. It may require some trial and error, but with knowledge, patience, and care, even the most challenging soils can be nurtured into productive ground.

Why Conduct a Garden Soil Test at Home?

Conducting a garden soil test at home is a crucial first step for any serious gardener or landscaper. The reason is simple: Your soil's health and properties directly impact the health and growth of your plants. Without the right balance of nutrients and the right pH level, your garden might not thrive as you would like it to. Furthermore, understanding the state of your soil can save you from unnecessary expenditures on fertilizers or amendments that your soil may not need. This is why conducting a garden-soil test at home is not only smart but also economical.

What Exactly Does the Soil Test Do?

A soil test does several things. It measures the texture of your soil (whether it's predominantly sandy, silty, or clay), the pH level, and the available amounts of nutrients such as magnesium, calcium, phosphorus, and potassium (Center for Agriculture, Food, and the Environment, 2015). Having this knowledge allows you to adjust your soil as needed to provide the best environment for your plants. Overapplication or under-application of nutrients can be harmful to your plants, so it's crucial to understand your soil's composition.

Reasons Why You Should Test the Garden Soil Before Planting

- **understanding nutrient levels:** By testing the soil, you'll be able to understand the level of essential nutrients present and what may need to be added for optimal plant growth.
- **determining pH level:** The pH level of your soil can drastically affect plant health. Some plants prefer more acidic soil, while others prefer it to be more alkaline.
- **identifying potential toxins:** Soil testing can help identify any possible contaminants in the soil, such as heavy metals or pollutants.
- **saving money:** By understanding your soil's specific needs, you can avoid wasting money on unnecessary soil amendments.
- **maintaining environmental friendliness:** Overuse of fertilizers can lead to runoff that contaminates local waterways. Testing your soil can help prevent over-fertilization.

How to Take a Soil Sample

Taking a soil sample is easy. Begin by removing any surface debris, like leaves or stones, from the area you want to sample.

Using a sanitized shovel or trowel, excavate a hole with a depth of 6–8 in. Within this hole, extract a soil slice that is 1 in. wide. From the center of this slice, eliminate a 1-in. strip. Repeat this process in different areas of your garden, combining the samples in a clean container. Allow the soil to dry, place it in a bag with your information. You can send this to a testing laboratory or your local extension office for analysis.

Simple In-House Soil Tests

There are several easy in-house soil tests you can do to gain a basic understanding of your soil's composition. These include:

Soil Texture Test

Also known as the jar test, this test involves placing a soil sample in a clear jar with water, shaking it well, and then letting it settle. The existence of various soil layers will offer valuable insights into the relative distribution of sand, silt, and clay particles.

Soil pH Test

A simple pH test involves adding vinegar to a soil sample. If it fizzes, the soil is alkaline. If not, add baking soda to a wet soil sample. If it fizzes, the soil is acidic. No reaction to either substance indicates neutral pH.

Earthworm Test

Earthworms are an excellent indicator of soil health. If you can find at least 10 earthworms in a cubic foot of soil, your soil is likely healthy.

Testing your garden soil before planting can save you time and money in the long run. By understanding the needs of your soil, you can create optimal conditions for your plants to thrive.

Texture

Soil texture pertains to the relative arrangement of sand, silt, and clay particles within a given volume of soil. These components determine how the soil will behave under different conditions—its water-holding capacity, its ability to retain nutrients, its ease of tillage, and many other properties that are crucial to plant growth.

Quick Field Tests to Determine Soil Texture

Quick field tests are useful methods to estimate your soil texture while on-site. These tests rely on the unique characteristics of sand, silt, and clay particles and the way they interact with water and with each other.

The Ribbon Test

Dampen a small amount of soil, then try to roll it into a thin ribbon between your thumb and forefinger. Sandy soils will crumble, silty soils will hold together but not form a long ribbon, and clay soils can be rolled into long, thin ribbons.

The Jar Test

As outlined in the previous section, the jar test involves mixing soil with water in a clear container and allowing it to settle. Subsequently, the distinct layers of sand, silt, and clay can be quantitatively measured.

Deciphering Soil Texture: Ranging From Fine to Coarse

The texture of the soil is usually outlined on a scale from fine to coarse, guided by the predominant soil particles. Fine-textured or clay-like soils, abundant in smaller particles like clay, provide a smooth feel. Medium-textured or loamy soils present a balance of sand, silt, and clay, giving a texture that's gritty yet somewhat smooth. Coarse-textured or sandy soils, filled with larger particles, offer a gritty sensation.

Classifying Soil Texture and Associated Field Tests

Soil texture is classified based on the relative distribution of sand, silt, and clay. The classification includes clay, silty clay, sandy clay, clay loam, silty clay loam, sandy clay loam, loam, silt loam, sandy loam, silt, sandy, and sand.

Several field tests can be used to classify your soil's texture, such as the ribbon test, jar test, and feel test, which involves rubbing moist soil between your fingers to gauge its smoothness or grittiness. You can then cross-reference your findings with the USDA soil triangle chart to pinpoint your soil's exact classification (Food and Agriculture Organization of the United Nations, n.d.).

Factors That May Impact Soil Test Results

Various elements can impact the results of soil tests. These include:

- The procedure and depth of soil collection, the season when the sample was gathered, and the consistency of the sample.

- Any recent amendments such as fertilizers or organic matter, the preceding crops, and the drainage condition.
- Variations in temperature, moisture content, and recent precipitation can modify soil chemistry and, in turn, affect test outcomes.
- Different laboratories may employ varying testing methods, which may lead to discrepancies in the results.

How Often Should I Test the Soil?

Testing your soil every 3–5 years is usually sufficient for maintaining a healthy garden or landscape. However, if you notice a decline in plant health or productivity, it may be useful to test sooner. More frequent testing may also be necessary if you are making significant changes to your soil, such as adding large amounts of compost, lime, or other amendments.

INTERACTIVE ELEMENT: INTERPRETING YOUR SOIL TESTING REPORT

You've done your due diligence by testing your soil, and now you've received your soil test report. This report is a gold mine of information about your soil's health, but how do you make sense of all the data? Don't worry. I'm here to guide you through this important process in a supportive, interactive way!

Reading the Report

First, let's focus on the primary elements of your report: pH levels, soluble salts, and nutrient levels. These may be presented with a series of numbers, often alongside a lab-specific range that categorizes these values from very low to extreme.

Understanding pH Values

The majority of greenhouse crops thrive within a relatively broad pH range. Your soil analysis should provide a pH reading, giving you an understanding of your soil's acidity or basicity.

Here are a few optimum pH ranges for your reference:

- Soilless substrates: 5.5–6.0
- Substrates containing 20% or more natural soil: 6.2–6.5 (Center for Agriculture, Food, and the Environment, 2015a)

If your soil's pH readings are below these optimum ranges, it implies your soil could be overly acidic. High acidity may result in deficiencies of essential nutrients such as calcium and magnesium. Additionally, it can lead to potentially toxic concentrations of certain micronutrients, like iron and manganese. A practical approach to resolving issues of low pH includes the incorporation of limestone prior to planting.

Understanding Soluble Salts

Next up is your soluble-salt level. This is a measure of the total dissolved salts in your soil, including nutrients like potassium, calcium, and magnesium. However, if levels are too high, these salts can inhibit plant growth.

Let's take a look at what the values could mean for your soil:

- Very low: 1:2 (0–0.03), saturated media extract (SME) (0–0.8), PourThru (0–1.0)
- Low: 1:2 (0.3–0.8), SME (0.8–2.0), PourThru (1.0–2.6)
- Normal: 1:2 (0.8–1.3), SME (2.0–3.5), PourThru (2.6–4.6)
- High: 1:2 (1.3–1.8), SME (3.5–5.0), PourThru (4.6–6.5)
- Very high: 1:2 (1.8–2.3), SME (5.0–6.0), PourThru (6.6–7.8)
- Extreme: 1:2 (>2.3), SME (>6.0), PourThru (>7.8)

Keep in mind that these ranges are lab specific. If your levels fall into the high or very high range, consider taking steps to reduce salinity, such as improving soil drainage or reducing the frequency of fertilizer application (Food and Agriculture Organization of the United Nations, n.d.-a).

Nutrient Levels

The analysis of your soil should provide an assessment of nutrient quantities. It should account for crucial macronutrients, including nitrogen, phosphorus, and potassium, alongside micronutrients, such as iron, manganese, and zinc. If the analysis reveals certain nutrient shortages, it may be necessary to fortify your soil with a targeted fertilizer or modify the soil pH to enhance the accessibility of nutrients.

Remember that the best interpretation of your soil-test report considers all aspects: The crop you're growing, its stage of development, your fertilization routine, and any crop problems you've observed.

Lastly, retest your soil every 3–5 years or whenever you notice changes in plant health. Soil is a dynamic medium that changes over time, and staying informed about its condition will support your gardening success!

CONCLUSION

We journeyed to the very roots of successful gardening and landscaping—the soil. Unearthing its mysteries, we familiarized ourselves with the various soil types and their unique characteristics, realizing that understanding and working with these differences are key to cultivating a thriving garden. We delved into the critical practice of soil testing, examining not only the reasons for its importance but also practical ways of conducting these tests at home and interpreting the results.

Our exploration underscored the value of a proactive approach to soil health, affirming Franklin D. Roosevelt's words, "The Nation that destroys its soil destroys itself." Equipped with this newfound knowledge, we are now ready to embark on the next stage of our journey, where we will utilize this knowledge to plan and create a drought-resistant landscape.

Preparing for the Future

"Climate change is sometimes misunderstood as being about changes in the weather. In reality, it is about changes in our very way of life."
— Paul Polman

The reality of climate change means that drought-resistant landscapes are going to become increasingly important. Right now, it's not something the average gardener thinks about, but the more our land changes, the more relevant the issue will become and the more people will need to know how to handle it.

I'd like to inspire more readers to work with drought resistance in mind before we get to that point — and now you're this far through our journey together, I'd like to ask for your help in spreading the word.

That doesn't mean you have to talk about it with everyone you meet (although, let's be honest, you're probably going to want to!). All I need from you is a few moments of your time and your willingness to leave your honest feedback on this book online.

That might not seem like much, but the more discussion there is on the subject, the more awareness is raised — and the more likely it is that those who are already interested in finding out about drought-resistant landscaping will find the guidance they're looking for.

By leaving a review of this book on Amazon, you'll show new readers where they can find all the information they need to make their landscaping projects truly sustainable.

Simply by leaving a short review, you'll lay down a footpath toward guidance in drought-resistant landscaping and inspire new readers to find out more.

Thank you for your support. The future is coming, and it's my hope that we'll not only be prepared, but excited about the innovative ways in which we can handle it.

5

PLANNING THE LANDSCAPE

C enturies ago, Sir John Denham beautifully encapsulated the essence of creation in a single line: "When any great design thou dost intend, Think on the means, the manner, and the end" (Quote Fancy, n.d.). This wisdom holds true as much for the tangible marvels of architecture as it does for the humble gardener contemplating their next green masterpiece.

Imagine, if you will, a familiar scene: Your garden, where a symphony of colors meets the gaze and the soft rustle of leaves whispers in the wind. Now, picture this garden under the harsh rays of a scorching summer, wilted and gasping for water. A dismal image, isn't it? But let me tell you: It doesn't have to be this way.

In this chapter, we delve into the art and science of planning water-wise landscapes, an essential step in our 3-P approach— prepare, plant, and preserve. We focus on two key factors that stand between your green space and drought-like conditions:

the soil beneath your feet and the design layout of your landscape.

We'll start by going under the surface, quite literally, into the world of soil preparation and amendment. You'll find out why adding sand to your soil to improve drainage might not be the best idea and learn the ins and outs of soil evaluation. We'll also provide checklists for soil evaluation specific to garden soils and lawns. And because we know those fertilizer labels can be baffling, we'll decode them for you and guide you on how to choose the right one.

Once we have enriched the earth, we'll step back to appreciate the broader canvas—the landscape itself. As we navigate this process, we'll explore how to reduce the need for water and maintenance through strategic planning and design. Whether you're contemplating how much grass you need or whether to incorporate turfgrass at all, we'll guide you through your options. Moreover, we'll help you understand how to effectively use non-irrigated turfgrass areas and much more.

Drawing insights from a diverse range of sources, from university research to real-world case studies, we'll guide you through everything from principles of xeriscaping and hydrozoning to ingenious techniques like permeable hardscaping. We'll visit the cool shadows of shade trees and discuss the importance of proper plant spacing. Together, we'll transform the notion of a drought-tolerant garden from an elusive dream into an achievable reality.

This chapter aims to empower you, the reader, with the tools and knowledge necessary to craft a sustainable, water-efficient landscape even under the unforgiving glare of the summer sun. By the end of this chapter, I want you to look at your garden and see not a bleak image of drought-stricken flora but a vibrant, resilient haven. A place where beauty thrives, rain or shine.

So, let's grab our garden gloves and dig in—into the soil, into the planning, and into a future where our gardens are as kind to our planet as they are to our senses. Here's to the gardeners who dare to dream, to the landscapes that inspire us, and to the journey we're about to embark on together.

HOW TO NOT SOIL YOUR LAWN

Creating a lush, verdant lawn requires more than just a simple sprinkle of seeds and daily watering. The secret to a thriving lawn lies beneath the surface, in the composition and health of your soil. So, to make your lawn the talk of the neighborhood, you need to understand the dynamics of soil preparation and amendment. This involves recognizing soil problems, choosing appropriate amendments, and monitoring the health of your soil consistently. Now, let's unpack this step-by-step guide to optimizing your soil and cultivating a magnificent lawn.

Understanding and Fixing Soil Problems

Every soil is unique, possessing a specific structure, texture, and nutrient composition. Sometimes, these characteristics may not be ideal for growing grass, manifesting in poor growth and the lackluster appearance of your lawn. Common soil problems include compaction, pH imbalances, poor nutrient availability, inadequate drainage, and infestations by soil pests. To fix these issues, we need to delve deeper into the cause of each problem and the suitable remedies.

The Role of Sulfur and Limestone Amendments

Maintaining the correct soil pH is paramount to the health of your lawn. Pertaining to your soil, pH constitutes a measurement reflecting its acidity or alkalinity level, and deviations from the optimal range are a point of concern. It can prevent your grass from absorbing essential nutrients. Sulfur and limestone are two common soil amendments used to correct pH imbalances. Sulfur decreases soil pH, making the soil more acidic, while limestone increases soil pH, making it more alkaline. Grass usually prefers slightly acidic soil, so if your soil test indicates a high pH, sulfur may be required, and vice versa.

Incorporating Organic Matter

One of the most transformative ways to improve your soil's health is the addition of organic matter. Organic matter consists of decomposed plant and animal material such as compost, manure, and leaf mold. These materials enrich your soil with nutrients, improve its structure and water-retention capacity, and promote the growth of beneficial soil organisms. Organic matter is a superfood for your soil and a powerful tool in your lawn-care arsenal.

Infiltration Testing

A crucial characteristic of a healthy lawn is its ability to drain water efficiently. Overly soggy lawns can lead to a host of issues, including root rot, disease proliferation, and nutrient leaching. Conversely, if the soil drains too rapidly, it may not retain enough water for grass roots to absorb. This is where infiltration testing comes in. This test will assess your soil's drainage capacity and help you take steps to strike the right balance between water retention and drainage.

There's a common misconception that adding sand to clay soils will improve their drainage. Unfortunately, instead of loosening up the clay, the sand tends to form compact structures, making the soil even more impervious to water. The remedy lies in adding organic matter, which improves the soil structure, making it more porous and thereby improving drainage.

Soil Evaluation

A thorough soil evaluation is key to determining the overall health of your soil. It's not just about nutrient levels or pH balance. A good soil evaluation involves looking at the physical characteristics of your soil, such as its texture and structure, the chemical aspects, like nutrient composition and pH, and the biological factors, including the presence of beneficial organisms. Regular soil evaluations help you stay informed about your soil's health and guide your soil-management practices.

Aeration

A compacted lawn can suffocate your grass, leaving it weak and prone to disease. Compacted soil can impede the penetration of water and nutrients and restrict root growth. Aeration is a simple yet effective solution to this problem. By removing small plugs of soil from your lawn, aeration allows water, nutrients, and air to better reach the root zone, encouraging healthy and vigorous growth.

Evidence and Remedies

In addition to physical evaluations, chemical evaluations are necessary to identify nutrient deficiencies or excesses, pH imbalances, or the presence of harmful substances. Soil tests provide this valuable information, allowing you to tailor your soil amendment practices to the specific needs of your soil.

Understanding Fertilizer Applications for Lawns

Not all fertilizers are created equal. The nutrients they provide, the form they come in, and their application rates can vary widely. One key skill for lawn-care enthusiasts is learning how to read a fertilizer bag. These labels provide information on the nutrient content of the fertilizer, specifically the ratio of nitrogen, phosphorus, and potassium. Understanding these values will help you choose the right fertilizer for your lawn's specific needs.

The Issue of Compaction

Soil compaction is a common issue in lawns, especially those that receive heavy foot traffic. Compacted soil has reduced pore spaces, restricting the movement of water, air, and nutrients. This can stunt your lawn's growth and result in weak, thin grass. Regular aeration and the addition of organic matter can help alleviate soil compaction, allowing your lawn to flourish.

High Soil Sodium

Excessive sodium in the soil can have a detrimental impact on your lawn's health. High sodium levels can degrade soil structure, inhibit nutrient uptake, and cause water imbalances. If you suspect or know that your soil has a high sodium level, gypsum, a common soil amendment, can be used to flush out the excess sodium.

Dealing with Layering

Layering in soil occurs when different soil types or materials stratify into distinct layers, hindering the movement of water, nutrients, and air. It can often occur when topsoil is added to a lawn without properly integrating it with the existing soil. To eliminate layering, integrate the layers by thorough tilling and consider adding organic matter to improve overall soil structure.

Excessive Salts

Excessive salts in the soil can create an inhospitable environment for your lawn. The presence of salts can cause water stress in plants, even in moist conditions, and lead to nutrient imbalances. If you notice white crusts on your soil or if your plants are struggling despite regular watering, you might have a salt problem. Leaching, a process of washing away excess salts with copious amounts of water, and improving soil structure can help mitigate this issue.

Soil Cracking

Soil cracking often indicates a high proportion of clay in your soil. As clay soils dry, they shrink and form cracks, which can be detrimental to your lawn's health. Incorporating organic matter into your soil can improve its ability to retain moisture and help prevent soil cracking.

Soil Crusting

Soil crusting occurs when a hard layer forms on the soil surface. This can be detrimental to your lawn, preventing seedlings from emerging and reducing water infiltration. To mitigate soil crusting, try adding organic matter or using mulch to protect the soil surface.

Understanding Soil Texture

The way your soil feels and behaves is determined by its texture, which depends on the amounts of sand, silt, and clay it contains. From nutrient availability to water-holding capacity, the soil texture plays a huge role in how well your lawn can grow. Loamy soils, which have an even mixture of sand, silt, and clay, are generally considered the best for lawns.

Thatch

Thatch refers to the accumulation of deceased and living grass shoots, stems, and roots forming a layer on the soil surface. While a small amount of thatch can be beneficial, providing a protective layer and contributing to soil organic matter, an overly thick thatch layer can create a barrier to water, nutrients, and air. Regular dethatching can help keep your lawn healthy.

Addressing Undesirable Minerals

Soil tests can sometimes reveal high levels of undesirable minerals, such as lead or arsenic. These are cause for concern as they can be harmful to both plant health and human health. Remedies could include soil replacement, phytoremediation (using plants to extract harmful substances), or the addition of specific soil amendments.

Optimizing Water-Holding Capacity

A good water-holding capacity ensures that your lawn has access to the water it needs to thrive, especially during dry spells. This characteristic of soil is closely linked to its texture and organic matter content. Adding organic matter to your soil can significantly improve its ability to retain water, reducing the need for frequent watering and helping your lawn withstand periods of drought.

PLANNING AND DESIGN FOR A DROUGHT-TOLERANT LANDSCAPE

Making a shift toward drought-tolerant landscaping, also known as xeriscaping, can save significant amounts of water, money, and time in the long run. It's a forward-thinking approach to landscape design, particularly applicable to areas like California, where water scarcity is a frequent concern. Let's delve into how you can create a water-efficient, visually appealing, and sustainable landscape.

Planning Ahead

Careful planning is the key to successful landscape design. Begin with a site plan, taking into account the topography, sun exposure, existing vegetation, and natural drainage patterns. Identify different zones in your yard (front, back, sides, and parkway) and consider their unique features and requirements. To save water, employ the principle of hydrozoning, which involves grouping plants with comparable water requirements together.

Incorporate principles of xeriscaping, focusing on water conservation through the use of drought-tolerant plants and efficient irrigation methods. This doesn't mean your landscape will lack visual appeal. On the contrary, many drought-tolerant plants offer vibrant colors and interesting textures that can make your garden stunning year-round.

How Much Grass Do You Need?

Traditional lawns can be water intensive. Consider how much grass you actually need. Limit turfgrass to functional areas for activities like playing or picnicking and choose species with lower water requirements. Steer clear of planting grass in narrow, small, or irregularly shaped areas that make efficient irrigation challenging. Where the grass isn't necessary, consider alternatives like ground covers, shrubs, or a mix of perennials and annuals that are more water wise and can add visual interest to your yard.

Good Choices Make Good Landscapes

Choose plant species native to your region or those adapted to similar climates. These plants are naturally suited to the local conditions and often require less maintenance and water than non-native species. Embrace diversity in your plant choices, including trees, shrubs, perennials, grasses, and succulents, each contributing different heights, textures, and colors to the overall landscape design.

Ensure proper plant spacing, giving plants ample room to grow. Not only does this promote healthy growth, but it also helps prevent diseases by improving air circulation.

The Fun Part

Use permeable hardscaping materials, such as gravel, pebbles, or permeable pavers, for patios, paths, and driveways to allow water to permeate the ground, reducing runoff and promoting natural irrigation.

Incorporate elements of visual interest such as ornamental grasses, large boulders, or a dry creek bed. These add texture and depth to your landscape while requiring minimal water.

For sunny areas, consider planting shade trees. They not only add aesthetic appeal but also help reduce water evaporation from the ground, keep your home cooler, and save water in the long run.

Irrigation

Efficient irrigation is a fundamental aspect of water-wise landscaping. The aim is to reduce water waste by ensuring water is applied where it's needed, at the right time, and in the right amount.

Drip irrigation systems are particularly effective in this regard. They deliver water directly to the plant's roots, minimizing evaporation and runoff. These systems are generally more water efficient than traditional sprinkler systems, as they allow for a more precise application of water.

Maintenance of the irrigation system is also crucial to keep it running efficiently. Regularly inspect the system for leaks or malfunctions and adjust your irrigation schedule according to the season and weather changes.

Mulch Application

Mulch serves several essential functions in a drought-tolerant landscape. It helps conserve soil moisture, reduces soil temperature fluctuations, prevents weed growth, and adds organic matter to the soil over time. For optimal results, add organic mulch at a depth of 3–4 in. or inorganic mulch at a depth of 2–3 in. Leave a small gap around the base of woody plants without mulch to avoid diseases and protect against rodent damage (Crawford & Cabrera, 2021).

Routine Maintenance

Maintenance is a crucial aspect of any landscape, traditional or water wise. This includes tasks like pruning, weeding, pest control, and fertilization. The beauty of a water-wise landscape is that, as it matures, by creating a more self-sustaining environment, you'll reduce the amount of time and effort needed for maintenance.

A drought-tolerant landscape not only conserves water but also invites a diverse ecosystem into your yard. Over time, you'll observe a variety of birds, insects, and wildlife drawn to the native plants and the habitat they provide. In the process, your yard will become an integral part of the local ecosystem, contributing positively to biodiversity.

Analysis of Landscape Examples

Let's take a closer look at a few landscapes and evaluate them from a water conservation perspective.

Typical Landscape

A typical landscape, often characterized by large expanses of lawns, can be quite water intensive. From a water conservation standpoint, this type of landscape is not ideal. Grass, especially if not native to the area, can require significant amounts of water to stay green and healthy. Additionally, the irrigation of such landscapes can be inefficient, leading to water wastage.

Water-Efficient Landscape

A water-efficient landscape focuses on minimizing water usage. Drought-tolerant plants, efficient irrigation systems, mulching, and appropriate plant grouping based on water needs (hydro-zoning) are all elements of such a landscape. This landscape is sustainable, aesthetically pleasing, and contributes positively to biodiversity.

Strolling Garden

A strolling garden, with its winding paths, varied plantings, and carefully designed vistas, can be adapted to a drought-tolerant ethos. By selecting water-wise plants, employing efficient irrigation, and integrating permeable hardscaping, such a garden can become an example of water conservation without compromising its inherent charm and tranquility.

Water-Wise Landscaping

Landscaping plays a significant role in the aesthetics and functionality of your home. However, with the increasing need for water conservation, many homeowners are looking for ways to create a beautiful landscape without draining water resources. This guide aims to provide you with key principles and practices to help you build a water-wise landscape, focusing on four main areas: the parkway, front yard, side yard, and backyard.

Parkway Landscaping

The parkway, or the strip of land between the sidewalk and the street, is often the first part of your property people notice. This area typically has high foot traffic and little shade, so opt for drought-resistant plants that can thrive under these conditions. Consider plants like succulents, which have a high tolerance for heat and can go for extended periods without water. Additionally, remember to avoid planting turfgrass in narrow or small areas as it can be challenging to irrigate efficiently.

Front Yard

The front yard sets the tone for your entire home. It should be visually appealing but also practical. Turfgrass can play a significant role here. It provides an excellent play area for kids, promotes soil health, and can help cool down your home during hot weather. When choosing turfgrass for a water-wise landscape, consider species with lower water requirements, such as buffalo grass or Bermuda grass. Additionally, consider hydrozoning—grouping plants with similar watering needs together—to optimize irrigation and conserve water.

Side Yard

The side yard, often a neglected space, acts as a transition between the front and backyards. With careful planning, this area can serve various functional and aesthetic purposes. You can plant shade trees to create a cool, relaxing path connecting the front- and backyard, and at the same time, save on water, as these trees can reduce water evaporation. Remember, though, that it's best to avoid planting turfgrass in hard-to-irrigate areas like these.

Backyard

The backyard is often where families spend the majority of their outdoor time. For a water-wise backyard, consider replacing traditional grass with drought-tolerant alternatives or creating a xeriscape garden. Xeriscaping is a landscaping method that utilizes native, drought-tolerant plants to minimize or eliminate the need for irrigation. Furthermore, use organic compost and mulch to improve plant health and insulate the roots from heat, leading to less water usage.

Remember to also create practical turf areas in your backyard where it's functional, like children's play areas or pet spaces. Again, choose turfgrass species with lower water needs and use cultural practices, like proper mowing and fertilization, to improve their water-use efficiency.

Enhancing Drought Resistance in Your Landscape

Apart from careful site planning and plant design, you can further improve the drought resistance of your landscape by embracing nature's resilience through xeriscaping, practicing hydrozoning, installing permeable hardscaping, properly spacing your plants, and opting for shade trees.

Xeriscaping

Xeriscaping uses native and drought-tolerant plants to create beautiful, resilient landscapes that need little to no irrigation. This approach is not only water wise but also environmentally friendly as it promotes local biodiversity.

Hydrozoning

Hydrozoning involves grouping plants with similar water needs together. This strategy makes watering more efficient and helps prevent overwatering or underwatering, which can harm both plants and waste water (Barrett, 2018).

Permeable Hardscaping

Permeable hardscapes, such as gravel paths or permeable pavers, allow rainwater to soak into the ground, reducing runoff and helping to replenish groundwater supplies.

Shade Trees

Shade trees can significantly reduce your landscape's water needs by providing shade that reduces water evaporation from the soil. Plus, they can create cool, comfortable outdoor spaces and reduce your home's cooling costs.

Proper Plant Spacing

Proper plant spacing ensures each plant has enough room to grow without competing for water and nutrients. It also improves air circulation, reducing the risk of disease that could weaken your plants and make them require more water.

By incorporating these principles into your landscaping strategy, you can enjoy a beautiful, functional outdoor space that's also water-wise and sustainable. Remember, every step you take toward water conservation is a step toward a more sustainable future.

Setting Your Lawn up for Drought Tolerance

It's important to condition your lawn for resilience against droughts. While drought can be damaging, you can reduce its impact on your garden with a few careful steps:

- **improve the soil:** Healthy soil is one of the most critical aspects of maintaining a drought-tolerant landscape. To enhance its structure and fertility, you can incorporate organic matter like compost or manure into the soil. This will help the soil retain moisture and provide a good environment for plant roots.
- **maintain proper mowing height:** Mowing your lawn at the correct height can reduce water loss and enhance root development. Leaving the grass a bit longer during dry periods provides shade for the roots and prevents the soil from drying out quickly.
- **leave mulch clippings:** Leaving grass clippings on the lawn after mowing can help improve soil quality and

conserve water. The clippings decompose quickly and return nutrients to the soil while reducing water evaporation from the lawn's surface.

• **aerate the soil:** Aeration can help your lawn absorb and retain more water by reducing soil compaction and making it easier for water and nutrients to reach the roots. This can be done with a simple garden fork or a specialized aeration tool.

• **avoid fertilizing during drought:** Applying fertilizer during a drought can stress your lawn, as it promotes growth that the grass may not be able to sustain without adequate water. Wait until normal rainfall resumes to fertilize your lawn.

Additional Drought Resilience

Trees and shrubs have an advantage over grass and other plants due to their typically deeper root systems, which can be especially beneficial during drought periods. This advantage allows them to access moisture from deeper layers of the soil, promoting better survival and resilience. However, they are not immune to drought stress and may need some additional care, so:

• Regularly prune your trees and shrubs to remove any dead or diseased branches and promote healthier growth.

• Deep water your trees and shrubs to encourage deep root growth, helping them access water from deeper soil layers.

- Mulch around the base of your trees and shrubs to retain soil moisture and reduce evaporation. This also helps keep the soil temperature consistent, which can be beneficial for root health.

Vacation Preparation

If you are planning a vacation during the dry season, it is important to prepare your garden to survive while you are away. Here are some tips:

- Install a drip irrigation system on a timer to water your plants regularly.
- Ask a neighbor or hire a professional gardener to water your plants while you are away.
- Mulch your garden to keep the soil moist for longer periods.
- If possible, move potted plants to shady areas to reduce water loss from evaporation.

With proper planning and a few changes to your gardening habits, you can cultivate a beautiful, thriving landscape that is more resilient to drought. By incorporating these tips and techniques, you can conserve water, protect your plants, and contribute to environmental sustainability.

CONCLUSION

In Chapter 5, we took you on a journey through the second part of the 3-P approach—planning and designing water-wise landscapes—preparing you to better manage drought-like conditions. We guided you from the foundations of soil preparation and amendment, offering solutions to typical soil problems, to the intricacies of designing a drought-tolerant landscape. We stressed the principles of water-wise landscaping and unveiled various landscaping techniques that cater specifically to water conservation. Key aspects like hydrozoning, permeable hardscaping, and xeriscaping were discussed, along with the importance of thoughtful plant spacing and choice of species. We also presented methods to prevent water runoff and concluded with a subtle introduction to the significance of mulching. By the end of this chapter, you, dear reader, have gained a strategic blueprint to create a landscape that's not only resilient and attractive but also water wise.

6

MULCHING IS COOL

> *"If garden requires it, now trench it ye may, one trench not a yard from another go lay: Which being well filled with muck by and by, go cover with mold for a season to lay."*

—Nouembers husbandry

In our quest for sustainable and beautiful landscapes, we've walked through the pathways of planting and pruning, and now it's time to put on our gloves again and get our hands dirty with mulching. This is an ancient gardening technique, as is beautifully captured in the 16th-century verse above, which encapsulates the age-old wisdom and time-tested methodology of this simple but transformative practice.

We've all been there, admiring a meticulously manicured garden or landscape and wondering how on earth it's kept looking so vibrant, fresh, and weed free. More often than not, the secret isn't some mystical gardening elixir but something much more accessible and practical: mulch.

To put it simply, mulching is like the icing on a cake, a top layer that seals in moisture, provides nutrients, deters weeds, and adds an aesthetic touch to your landscape. This chapter serves as a comprehensive guide to understand not only why mulching matters but also how to do it effectively to bring your landscape to life.

The many benefits of mulching are more than meets the eye, going deep below the surface to work wonders on your garden's health and resilience. From moisture conservation to enhancing fertility and even remedying heavy metals, mulching is a miracle worker. It might surprise you to learn that the right mulch can even mitigate salt stress, aid in plant growth and development, and even have economic importance due to its comparative advantages.

Don't be disheartened by the few potential downsides of mulching; we'll guide you on how to navigate and minimize these pitfalls. Whether you're facing issues related to soil erosion, weed inhibition, or nutrient supply, there's a mulching solution out there for you.

And it's not all about the practical benefits. A well-chosen and properly applied mulch can visually enhance your landscape, serving as the finishing touch that brings your gardening vision to life.

As we delve deeper, we'll explore different types of mulch—from organic to inorganic—and give you the lowdown on their respective pros and cons. This practical guide will walk you through the mulching process, showing you how to prepare the surface, when to apply mulch, and even when to avoid it.

With easy-to-follow guides and expert tips, you'll be well-equipped to "mulch like you mean it." We'll explore best practices, dos and don'ts, and even offer video guides for those who learn best by watching. By the end of this chapter, you'll know not only the what's and whys of mulching but also the how's.

But before we dive in, remember: Mulching, like any good gardening practice, is as much about the journey as it is about the destination. Take your time, enjoy the process, and remember that every handful of mulch you lay down is a step toward a healthier, happier, and more sustainable landscape. Let's embark on the next stage of our journey. Exploring how to design your landscape in ways that reduce water runoff and waste, leading us to the third "P" of our 3-P approach: preserve.

Now, grab your gardening gloves. It's time to get mulching!

MULCHING

Landscaping is more than just an aesthetic pursuit. It's about creating a vibrant, healthy ecosystem that promotes biodiversity and sustainability. One of the most underappreciated yet pivotal tools in this endeavor is mulch. Through its plethora of benefits, mulching significantly aids in transforming your garden into an environmental powerhouse, thereby revolutionizing the way you garden. This comprehensive guide will delve into the reasons behind the essentiality of mulching, its potential advantages in both agriculture and environmental management, and the economic importance of mulching.

The Magic of Mulch

Mulch is a layer of material applied to the surface of the soil. Various organic materials, such as compost, bark chips, and straw, or inorganic materials, like gravel and plastic, can serve as mulch. This simple but effective technique offers an array of benefits. It conserves soil moisture, minimizes soil compaction and erosion, regulates soil temperature, and improves soil fertility (Tiwari, 2020). Additionally, mulch can mitigate salt stress, promote plant growth and yield, diminish diseases, and decrease the occurrence of weeds.

The Agricultural Benefits of Mulching

Water is the lifeblood of any garden, and its conservation is crucial. Mulching helps conserve soil moisture by reducing evaporation from the soil surface, limiting water usage while ensuring your plants get the hydration they need. The preserved moisture also contributes to maintaining a soil structure that fosters root development.

Minimization of Soil Compaction and Erosion

A bare, exposed garden is at the mercy of natural elements. Rain, particularly heavy downpours, can compact and erode soil, impacting plant health. Mulch acts as a protective shield, absorbing the impact of rain and minimizing the risk of soil compaction and erosion.

Regulation of Soil Temperature

Just like us, plants appreciate a stable temperature. Mulch acts as an insulating layer, keeping the soil cool during scorching summer days and warm during chilly winter nights. This temperature regulation can extend the growing season and protect your plants from temperature shocks.

Improvement of Soil Fertility

Organic mulches like compost or bark chips gradually decompose, enriching the soil with nutrients. This natural fertilization method can enhance the soil structure, improve its water-holding capacity, and boost its overall fertility, making it a nurturing environment for plant growth.

Mitigation of Salt Stress, Disease Diminution, and Weed Decline

High salt levels in the soil can be detrimental to plant health. Mulch helps mitigate salt stress by reducing evaporation and, thus, salt accumulation on the soil surface. Additionally, it creates a physical barrier between the plant and disease spores present in the soil, thereby decreasing the risk of diseases. Lastly, by blocking sunlight, mulch prevents weed germination, curbing their growth without resorting to harmful herbicides.

Mulching for Environmental Management

Aside from its agricultural benefits, mulching also plays a crucial role in environmental management.

Remediation of Heavy Metals

Certain types of mulch, particularly those made from organic materials, can help bind heavy metals present in the soil, preventing them from entering the food chain.

Diminishment of Pesticide Use

By suppressing weed growth and reducing plant diseases, mulch can lower the reliance on chemical herbicides and pesticides, contributing to a healthier and more sustainable environment.

Visual Enhancement

Mulch also serves an aesthetic purpose. It provides a neat, finished look to gardens and landscapes, adding to the visual appeal of your outdoor spaces.

Economic Importance of Mulching

Mulching not only contributes to a healthier environment but also makes economic sense. The use of mulch can reduce the need for water, fertilizers, and pesticides, thereby saving on these costs. Furthermore, healthier plants and improved yields can translate into higher profits for farmers and gardeners.

Comparatively, un-mulched soil tends to lose moisture quickly, requires more frequent watering, and is prone to weed infestation and erosion, all contributing to increased maintenance costs. Thus, a small investment in mulch can reap significant economic benefits in the long run.

Although mulching offers numerous benefits, it is crucial to be aware of potential drawbacks. If applied improperly, mulch can cause issues such as waterlogging, attracting pests, or creating a habitat for rodents. However, with proper application and management, these disadvantages can be avoided.

Mulch: A Garden's Best Friend

Mulch provides valuable nutrients to the soil while inhibiting weeds, preventing soil erosion, and enhancing the aesthetic appeal of your garden. It's a cost-effective, sustainable, and easy-to-apply solution for various gardening challenges.

By understanding the whys and how's of mulching, gardeners and landscapers can effectively use this technique to nurture vibrant, resilient, and sustainable green spaces. A mulched garden is not just a thriving garden but a testament to responsible and informed gardening. Happy mulching!

MULCH LIKE YOU MEAN IT

Mulching is one of the most beneficial practices a gardener can adopt. It's an inexpensive, easy-to-do task that has multiple benefits, including water retention, weed suppression, soil temperature regulation, and aesthetic enhancement of the landscape. However, for the full benefits to be realized, mulching should be done thoughtfully and thoroughly. Let's delve deeper into the world of mulch, exploring different types, best practices for application, and things to avoid.

Preparing for a Dry Winter

Preparing your garden for a dry winter is crucial. With climate changes causing unpredictable weather patterns, we can't solely rely on snow or rain to provide adequate moisture. Mulching is a beneficial practice that can help your plants survive through a dry winter.

Mulching in late autumn, after the first hard frost, can help to insulate the soil, maintaining a more consistent soil temperature and reducing the rate of heat loss. A layer of mulch can also help to retain moisture in the soil, preventing the desiccation that can occur due to cold, dry winter winds.

Applying Mulch

Proper application of mulch is key. The layer of mulch should be 2–3 in. thick. This thickness is enough to deter weeds, retain moisture, and maintain temperature, without the risk of suffocating plant roots or promoting rot. The mulch should also not be applied directly against the stems or trunks of plants, as this can cause damage or disease.

When mulching around trees, be sure not to pile mulch against the trunk. This practice, known as "volcano mulching," can lead to a host of issues, including promoting disease and rot, attracting pests, and suffocating the tree.

Mulch Types

The right type of mulch for your garden will depend on various factors, including your specific plants' needs, the climate, and your aesthetic preference. There are several types of mulch to consider.

Organic Mulch

Organic mulch is made from natural materials that decompose over time, improving the soil's fertility and structure.

Compost

Compost makes a great mulch and adds a lot of nutrients to the soil, but it isn't as effective at deterring weeds. Be sure that your compost pile gets hot enough to kill weed seeds to avoid encouraging weed growth.

Bark Mulch

Bark mulch or wood chips, including rubber bark, are widely used because of their availability and affordability. These mulches are good at suppressing weeds and retaining moisture but don't contribute as many nutrients to the soil as other organic mulches.

Straw

Straw is light, easy to spread, and decomposes relatively quickly, releasing nutrients into the soil. It is a popular choice for vegetable gardens.

Leaves

Leaves can be shredded and used as mulch. They decompose relatively quickly and add nutrients back into the soil.

Cardboard

Cardboard, paper, or burlap can also be used as mulch. While these materials don't add nutrients to the soil, they are excellent at weed suppression and moisture retention.

Other plant matter, like grass clippings or pine needles, can also be used as mulch. Grass clippings are effective but can get mucky if piled too deep. Pine needles are long lasting and great for acid-loving plants like azaleas, as they acidify the soil.

Inorganic Mulch

Inorganic mulches are made from man-made materials or non-decomposable natural materials.

Gravel

Gravel, stone, or rock are long-lasting and require minimal maintenance. They don't contribute to the soil's fertility but are good for decorative purposes and for use in areas where little to no digging is required.

Plastic

Plastic sheeting or landscape fabric is excellent at weed control and moisture retention. However, they don't allow water and air to penetrate the soil effectively, which can affect soil health over time.

Pros and Cons

Every type of mulch comes with its advantages and drawbacks. It's important to consider these when choosing the right mulch for your garden.

- Compost: great for soil nutrition but may encourage weed growth.
- Bark mulch or wood chips: good for weed suppression and moisture retention but low in nutrient addition.
- Straw: decomposes quickly, adding nutrients to the soil but may attract pests.
- Gravel, stone, or rock: low maintenance but doesn't contribute to soil fertility.
- Leaves: add nutrients to the soil but decompose quickly.
- Cardboard, paper, or burlap: excellent for weed suppression and moisture retention but offer no nutrient addition.
- Other plant matter: nutrient-rich but can create a mucky mess if overused.
- Plastic sheeting or landscape fabric: great for weed control but poor water and air penetration.

When to Avoid Mulch (or Go Light on It)

Mulch is generally beneficial, but there are situations when it's better to go light on it or avoid it altogether. For example, if you're planting seeds, you don't want to cover the area with thick mulch, as this could hinder the germination process. Similarly, avoid mulching when the soil is overly wet or if pests or diseases are present, as the mulch could exacerbate these issues.

When to Apply Mulch

While there's no perfect time to apply mulch, there are times that are generally more beneficial. For example, mulching in the spring can help suppress weeds and retain moisture for the dry summer months. Mulching in late fall, after the soil has frozen, can help protect plant roots from harsh winter conditions.

What Type of Garden Mulch Should I Use?

The type of mulch you use will depend on the needs of your garden. Consider your plants' specific needs, the climate, and your garden's aesthetic when making your choice.

Dos and Don'ts

- Do mulch in late fall or early spring.
- Don't pile mulch against the stems or trunks of plants.
- Do apply a 2–3-in. layer of mulch.
- Don't mulch as a quick fix for poor soil. Prioritize improving your soil's fertility and structure before mulching.
- Do consider the specific needs of your plants when choosing a mulch type.

Mulching is an essential garden task that provides numerous benefits. It's a simple way to enhance the health and appearance of your garden. By understanding the different types of mulch and the correct application techniques, you can provide your garden with a boost that will keep it thriving all year round.

Mulching, an essential gardening practice, can breathe new life into your landscape, particularly during drought conditions. It's more than just a means to beautify your outdoor space—it's a lifeline for your plants. Mulch offers a myriad of benefits for your garden. Firstly, it helps in conserving moisture by reducing water evaporation, significantly lowering your need for regular watering. It also plays a vital role in soil management. For instance, it can break up heavy clay soils, enhancing water and air movement. In sandy soils, it helps improve nutrient retention and water-holding capacity.

During the sweltering summer months, mulch acts as a soil insulator, keeping your plant roots cooler. Furthermore, it's an effective way to suppress weed growth, and if any weeds do sprout, they're typically easier to remove.

Mastering Lawn Mulching: The Correct Way

To maximize the benefits of mulching, keep these crucial considerations in mind:

- **initiation:** Prior to putting down mulch, it's essential to eliminate all existing weeds and to adequately moisten the designated area.
- **underneath trees:** Replace the grass beneath trees with mulch to minimize the fight for vital water and nutrients.
- **proximity to base:** Keep a clearance of 6–12 in. from the base of trees and shrubs free of mulch to circumvent possible decay and pest infiltration.
- **thickness:** Distribute a layer of mulch approximately 2–4 in. deep throughout all planted areas. Fine mulches should have a maximum depth of 2 in., while coarser materials like bark chunks can be as thick as 4 in.

Choosing the Perfect Mulch

Mulch can be purchased either bagged or in bulk quantities, which are quantified in cubic yards. To determine the amount of mulch you require, use this straightforward formula: Multiply the area (in square feet) by the depth (in parts of feet, not inches), then divide by 27.

CONCLUSION

As we wrap up this pivotal chapter on mulching, we've explored the multidimensional benefits of this time-tested gardening technique. Mulching isn't just a necessity; it's a statement of your commitment to a thriving, sustainable garden. With potential advantages ranging from soil-moisture conservation and temperature regulation to enhancing aesthetic appeal and mitigating environmental stressors, the benefits of mulching are manifold. We've also delved into the assortment of mulch types, both organic and inorganic, and best practices for their application, illuminating the path to a well-mulched garden.

Despite a few disadvantages, the rewards of mulching far outweigh the minor drawbacks. However, remember that mulching isn't a once-off task; it's a cyclic process that requires your regular attention to maintain the health and vibrancy of your landscape.

Now, having mastered the art of mulching, we're ready to venture further into the garden, embracing other ways to reduce water runoff and waste, a vital consideration in landscape design. This leads us neatly into the third "P" of our 3-P approach, an exciting journey yet to unfold.

7

LANDSCAPING WITH THE FLOW

> "Tis rushing now adown the spout,/ And gushing out below,/ Half frantic in its joyousness,/ And wild in eager flow./ The earth is dried and parched with heat,/And it hath long to be/ Released from the selfish cloud,/ To cool the thirsty tree."
>
> —Elizabeth Oakes Smith

Just as a bird flutters its wings to dance in the rain, we too can enjoy a symbiotic relationship with our environment. Consider the journey of a raindrop: It's born in the vast expanse of the clouds, dives to the earth, quenches the thirst of the living world, and eventually returns to the sky to start the cycle anew. This continual exchange between the earth and the heavens is nature's version of renewable energy. We can draw inspiration from this and take steps to harness the power of this cycle for ourselves. This chapter explores how to do just that, from harvesting rainwater to wisely managing runoff, show-casing the union of human ingenuity and natural abundance.

The way water moves in a landscape—rolling off roofs, soaking into the soil, being used by plants—isn't too dissimilar to how life ebbs and flows. As a permaculture enthusiast, you can learn to dance with this natural rhythm by collecting and using rain-water, a practice called rainwater harvesting. Let's dissect the who, what, and why of this system: Is it for you, how does it work, and why is it worth doing?

Rainwater harvesting is a remarkable way to become more water independent, reduce the strain on local water resources, and keep our gardens thriving, even in the face of increasingly frequent droughts. The process starts with simple observation and understanding of your landscape, employing a set of eight guiding principles. These principles help us not only collect and store water but also create an environment that is water wise and self-sustaining.

Of course, successfully implementing a rainwater-harvesting system isn't as simple as setting out a bucket and waiting for a downpour. You must take into account the unique characteristics of your property: the watershed, the flow of water, and rainfall calculations. These factors require a thoughtful assessment of your landscape and your needs. While a professional might bring additional expertise, don't let that deter you from getting your hands dirty. Later in the chapter, we'll introduce a DIY project using recycled materials that you can try yourself.

Managing water runoff is another crucial aspect of water conservation. The runoff from rain events is a precious resource that can be harnessed for multiple uses in our gardens and homes. We'll dive into the discussion of earthworks specifically designed to conserve and manage this runoff. Think of it as a natural savings account for water, steadily building up a reserve that can be tapped into when needed.

Specific techniques, such as creating berms and swales, sunken beds, and waffle gardens, allow us to direct and store runoff in a way that benefits our landscape and our water bills. We'll guide you step by step through these methods, using a range of excellent resources and helping you become your own water steward.

Like the rain that we're learning to harvest, this chapter aims to nourish your understanding of water conservation. Each segment, like each droplet, builds upon the last to create a holistic view of water management in permaculture. So, let's step out, open our arms wide, and welcome the rain. The dance begins here.

THE IMPORTANCE OF RAINWATER HARVESTING

Water is a precious resource and the lifeblood of our planet. Today, however, due to multiple factors such as rapid urbanization, high personal consumption levels, and a changing climate, clean water supplies are under significant strain. As a result, sustainable water-management practices have become more important than ever before. One such practice is rainwater harvesting, a primary element of integrated urban water management. This section will delve into the concept, history, and significance of rainwater harvesting, illuminating its crucial role in combating current and future water challenges.

The Basics

Rainwater collection is the practice of gathering and storing rainwater before it spreads out as surface runoff. This typically involves intercepting the water flowing off a rooftop and guiding it toward a storage container. The gathered rainwater, renowned for its exceptional quality, can be put to use for various non-drinking purposes. These include flushing toilets, doing laundry, watering gardens, and washing vehicles. By retaining and recycling rainwater, this method eases the load on municipal water facilities and infrastructure.

History of Rainwater Harvesting

The practice of rainwater harvesting is not new. Evidence of rainwater collection can be traced back thousands of years to ancient civilizations. Ancient Romans, for instance, collected rainwater in simple clay pots or cisterns. In different parts of the globe, such as the arid landscapes of the Middle East, sophisticated systems of rainwater capture, storage, and distribution were built to support agriculture and human survival.

Over time, the methods and technologies used for rainwater harvesting have evolved and improved. Today, rainwater harvesting is being adopted on a broader scale as part of integrated urban water-management strategies. It is seen not only as a solution to water scarcity but also as a tool for flood control, environmental conservation, and sustainable urban development.

Conservation of Water Resources

Rainwater harvesting reduces our reliance on conventional water sources such as groundwater and reservoirs. As we face a future with strained water resources, every drop of water saved through rainwater harvesting can contribute significantly to water conservation efforts. In the UK, reusing rainwater has been shown to reduce mains water consumption in commercial applications by up to 80% and around 55% in domestic homes (Kingspan, n.d.). In certain countries, this percentage can be even higher, showcasing the significant potential for water conservation.

Reducing Flood Risks and Managing Stormwater

An often-overlooked benefit of rainwater harvesting is its role in flood-risk reduction. The system operates by gathering water from on-site roof areas and directing the recycled water through appliances to the foul system instead of the storm drains. This approach effectively reduces peak flow rates. It can also help manage stormwater, easing the strain on stormwater infrastructure and reducing the impact on the environment. This can be particularly beneficial in urban areas where the infrastructure may not be equipped to handle heavy stormwater loads.

Economic Benefits

Rainwater harvesting can lead to significant cost savings for homeowners and businesses, particularly those who have water meters. Using harvested rainwater for non-potable uses reduces reliance on metered water, leading to lower water bills.

Additionally, sustainable features such as rainwater-harvesting systems can increase property values as there is growing consumer demand for green and sustainable homes.

Promoting Urban Sustainability and Resilience

Harvested rainwater can provide a sustainable source of water for urban green spaces, which play a vital role in maintaining healthy urban environments. Integrating rainwater harvesting into urban design can contribute to the creation of livable, productive, and resilient cities.

Rainwater harvesting plays a crucial role in sustainable water management, environmental protection, and urban resilience. As we face an era of increasing water challenges, the importance of rainwater harvesting will only continue to grow. It's therefore imperative that architects, designers, builders, and homeowners consider incorporating rainwater harvesting into their projects and homes, contributing to a more sustainable and water-secure future.

COLLECTING WATER FROM HEAVEN

Water is life, a fundamental resource that sustains our planet and its diverse life forms. The potential of harnessing this essential element, particularly from an unlikely source such as the sky, offers an exciting premise. With the advent of rainwater-harvesting techniques, we now have the means to capture, store, and utilize precipitation from heaven. This guide introduces the concept, principles, and various techniques of rainwater harvesting, helping you embark on a journey to sustainable water management.

Rainwater harvesting is the collection and storage of rainwater for direct use or future purposes. This age-old practice offers a plethora of benefits, such as lowering water bills, lessening dependence on water supply systems, mitigating floods and droughts, and replenishing groundwater levels. Rainwater is a clean, free, and sustainable source of water, and with the right harvesting techniques, we can harness its potential to a remarkable extent.

The Eight Principles of Rainwater Harvesting

Navigating the world of rainwater harvesting begins with understanding its eight key principles. These principles are designed to ensure efficient, safe, and sustainable harvesting.

Begin With Long and Thoughtful Observation

Before embarking on any rainwater-harvesting project, it's essential to observe your surroundings carefully. Understanding the local climate, landscape, and water dynamics is critical for developing an effective plan.

Start at the Top and Work Down

Always start at the highest point of your property and work your way down. This strategy allows you to leverage gravity to direct water flow, thereby minimizing the need for additional power sources.

Start Small and Simple

Begin with basic harvesting techniques before advancing to complex ones. Starting small enables you to learn from experience, gradually increasing your understanding of rainwater harvesting.

Spread and Infiltrate

To maximize the benefits of rainwater, ensure it's spread evenly and allowed to infiltrate the ground. This approach minimizes erosion and improves groundwater recharge.

Always Plan for Overflow

Even with the best intentions, rainwater systems can be overwhelmed during heavy rainfalls. Therefore, always incorporate overflow mechanisms to manage excess water.

Maximize Living, Organic Ground Cover

Living, organic ground cover helps absorb rainwater, prevent erosion, and enhance soil quality. It also acts as a natural filter for harvested rainwater.

Stack Functions to Maximize Beneficial Relationships and Efficiency

Utilize components of your rainwater-harvesting system to serve multiple functions. For instance, a pond could double as a water reservoir and a habitat for aquatic life.

Continually Reassess the Feedback Loops

Regularly assess your system's effectiveness and adjust as necessary. Observation and adaptation are key to the successful and sustainable implementation of rainwater-harvesting techniques.

Assessing Your Rainwater-Harvesting Potential

Before initiating a rainwater-harvesting project, it's vital to evaluate your property's potential for rainwater collection.

Know Your Watershed

Understanding your local watershed is critical. This includes knowledge of precipitation patterns, topography, soil characteristics, and existing water resources.

Map the Flow

Chart out the flow of water across your property. Identify high points, low points, and areas where water accumulates or drains away.

Calculate the Rainfall

Determine the average annual rainfall in your area. This data will inform the size and capacity of your rainwater-harvesting system.

Work Out the Runoff

Assess the amount of rainwater that could potentially be harvested from your property. This involves considering the size and material of your catchment area (roofs, pavements, etc.) and the local rainfall pattern.

Think About Your Water Needs

Evaluate your water requirements. Consider the needs of your garden, household, livestock, and any other uses for water on your property.

Rainwater-Harvesting Techniques

Infiltration Basins

These are shallow depressions that surround an anchor plant, usually a mature tree. The basin captures rainwater and allows it to infiltrate the ground, ensuring a steady supply of water to the plant. A basin's design encourages water flow into it and discourages mosquito breeding by ensuring complete infiltration within 12 hours.

Sunken Beds

These garden beds are dug downward into the soil and filled with mulch. The concept is particularly useful in areas with little rainfall or places with extreme rainfall seasons. Sunken beds help manage the rainwater effectively by capturing runoff from adjacent raised beds or pathways.

Waffle Gardens

This method involves cutting square-shaped beds into the ground. These "waffles" are then filled with mulch to create good-quality soil for plant growth. The design is particularly beneficial in arid climates, where the walls between the waffles insulate the soil and prevent plant freezing.

THE FUTURE OF WATER MANAGEMENT: EMBRACE RAINWATER HARVESTING

As we continue to grapple with increasing temperatures and water scarcity, rainwater harvesting presents a promising solution. It promotes water security, conserves a vital resource, and fosters a more sustainable future. While the journey to rainwater harvesting may seem complex, remember that each small step contributes to a significant impact on your water-management efforts. It's time we looked up to heaven, not just for inspiration but for a valuable resource that falls right into our hands—rainwater.

Conservatory Earthworks for Runoff Management

The beauty of our planet is derived from the fact that every natural element plays its part in maintaining the balance of life. Water, especially, is a critical player in the game. When it comes to effective water management, we need to look at one of nature's most generous gifts: rainwater. An effective and sustainable way to capture and use this precious resource is through rainwater harvesting. In this discussion, we'll focus on conservatory earthworks, particularly berms and swales, to manage runoff and promote the passive use of rainwater.

Understanding Berms and Swales

Berms and swales are ingenious earthworks commonly used in permaculture designs. A swale is essentially a shallow, wide ditch designed to capture and slow down the flow of water across a landscape, soaking it into the ground, replenishing groundwater levels, and making it available for plants. A berm is a raised mound of earth typically created on the downhill side of a swale, filled with organic matter, and planted with vegetation, usually trees, shrubs, and other perennials. Together, they work harmoniously to catch and store water, prevent soil erosion, and improve the fertility and hydration of the soil, making it ideal for a food forest.

Berms and swales are not just about water conservation. They play an integral role in landscape regeneration, transforming degraded lands into lush, productive ecosystems. By slowing down the speed at which water moves across the landscape, these earthworks reduce erosion and sediment loss, improve water infiltration, and increase groundwater recharge.

Step 1: Import a Contour Map Into Google Earth

The key to designing effective swales is to understand the topography of your land. Thankfully, technology comes to our rescue with tools like Google Earth. Google Earth can help you design swales by providing a visual representation of your landscape overlaid with contour lines, representing the earth's surface.

Begin by importing a contour map of your property into Google Earth. You can create a contour map using a web app like Contour Map Creator. Follow the steps below:

1. Locate your property on the Contour Map Creator website.

2. Draw a sampling area around your property by marking a rectangle with two pins on the map.
3. Generate a contour map using the "Get Data" button. Adjust the plot options to have contours every 15 ft or less, as required.
4. Download the contour map (KML file) and open it on Google Earth.

With the contour lines visible on the satellite photo background of your property, you can now design your swales.

Step 2: Outline Swales

To outline swales, follow the contours of the land and design on-contour ditches. The first swale, or the reference row, should ideally be at the highest point of the area of interest to slow down the water flow as soon as possible. Mark this initial swale using the "Add path" tool in Google Earth.

Then, decide the distance between subsequent swales based on site goals and rainfall and runoff conditions. The rule of thumb is: The greater the runoff, the closer the swales should be spaced. On gentle slopes with thick native grass, you'll need fewer and more widely spaced swales. On steep, overgrazed, or disturbed land with large volumes of fast-moving water during rainfalls, your swales should be placed at close intervals.

Follow these steps to create the final layout:

1. Use the "Ruler" tool in Google Earth to measure the desired distance to the next swale.

2. Use the "Add path" tool to draw a swale line following the contour line at the measured distance.
3. Repeat the process until you outline all swales.

In about 15 minutes, you can have a layout ready to be implemented on your site. You can save your work on Google Earth and visualize your layout as you walk around the site using the mobile app. While the Contour Map Creator isn't the most accurate tool for the job, it provides a good starting point for you to move your project forward.

The power to conserve water, reduce soil erosion, and transform landscapes lies in your hands. Using simple techniques like berms and swales can make a huge difference in how we interact with and shape our environment. Start implementing these techniques today to ensure our water security and contribute to a healthier planet.

Swales in Permaculture

Permaculture is a design philosophy that seeks to mimic the sustainable and resilient patterns found in natural ecosystems. One such pattern often replicated in permaculture designs is the water-harvesting swale. A swale is a horizontal trench dug along the contour line of a landscape. Its purpose is to slow down the movement of rainwater, allowing it to infiltrate the soil rather than running off the surface. This helps to prevent erosion, increases water availability for plants, and can recharge groundwater.

Let's dive into the step-by-step process of building a permaculture swale.

Step 1: Observe Water on Your Site

The first step in building a swale is to observe how water moves on your site. You can do this by watching the flow of water during heavy rain. Look for areas where water collects or where it flows quickly, causing erosion. These are potential areas where a swale might be beneficial. Note the general slope of the land and consider the sun orientation and shading patterns. All these aspects will impact the location and design of your swale.

Step 2: Identify the Ideal Site for a Permaculture Swale

After observing the water flow, the next step is to identify the ideal location for the swale. It should ideally be located where it will capture and hold the most water. This could be along a slope where water tends to run down, or it could be an area where water naturally collects. Keep in mind the proximity to plants and trees that could benefit from the increased water and ensure that the swale won't direct water toward buildings or other structures.

Step 3: Mark the Contour Line

Once you've identified the ideal location, you'll need to mark the contour line. This is the line along which you'll dig your swale. To find the contour line, you can use a tool like a water level or a laser level. This step is crucial because digging along the contour ensures the swale will be level and distribute water evenly across its entire length.

Step 4: Dig a Trench Along the Marked Contour Line

The next step is to dig a trench along the marked contour line. The size of the trench will depend on the amount of water you are trying to capture and the size of your site (Amy, 2014). Generally, the trench should be wide and shallow rather than narrow and deep. This allows the water to spread out and infiltrate more efficiently. Use a flat spade or a shovel to dig the trench and ensure the bottom is level.

Step 5: Mound the Soil to Create a Berm

While digging, pile the excavated soil on the downhill side of the trench to form a berm. The berm serves as a barrier that stops the flow of water, causing it to fill up the swale before overflowing across the surface of the berm. This effectively creates a temporary pond, giving the water time to infiltrate the soil. The berm also creates a raised planting area that can benefit from the extra moisture.

Step 6: Test and Adjust the Swale

After you've dug the trench and created the berm, it's time to test the swale. You can do this by running water into the swale and observing how it behaves. The water should spread evenly along the swale and not pool in one area. If you notice any areas where the water isn't spreading evenly, adjust the level of the trench as necessary.

Step 7: Plant the Swale

Now it's time to plant the swale. The type of plants you choose will depend on your climate, soil, and the needs of your landscape. Often, swales are planted with fruit trees, berry bushes, or other perennials that can take advantage of the extra moisture. Additionally, deep-rooted plants can help to break up compacted soil and improve water infiltration.

Step 8: Build Redundancy Into the Swale System

In permaculture, redundancy is a strategy that builds resilience into a system by duplicating critical functions. For swales, this might mean building more than one swale, each one capturing and infiltrating water if the one above it becomes overwhelmed. This not only increases the water-holding capacity of your landscape but also reduces the risk of water damage or erosion.

Step 9: Add Aesthetic Details

The final step is to add aesthetic details to your swale system. This could involve adding stepping stones for easy access, creating a wildflower meadow on the berm, or planting attractive ground covers that also act as living mulch. One attractive and functional detail to consider is the creation of sunken beds and waffle gardens, especially for those in arid climates.

Sunken Beds and Waffle Gardens

Sunken beds and waffle gardens are a unique water-conservation strategy, particularly suitable for arid regions. They have been successfully utilized by Indigenous communities, such as the Zuni Pueblo in New Mexico, for centuries. These methods work on a simple principle: Instead of raising beds above the ground level, as commonly done in many gardens, the beds are sunken or "dug in." This approach has several benefits tied to water conservation, climate resilience, and sustainable agriculture.

What Is a Sunken Bed?

In essence, a sunken bed is a garden bed that is dug into the ground rather than raised above it. This method is particularly beneficial in arid or desert-like climates where water scarcity is an issue. Sunken beds allow the plants to be at a level where they can easily access moisture, the soil stays cooler, and evaporation is reduced.

The Waffle Garden

A waffle garden is a type of sunken-bed garden, so named because it resembles a waffle's grid pattern. It is a series of small, square depressions surrounded by soil berms, much like the squares of a waffle. The berms help to keep the moisture in the planted depressions, making waffle gardens a highly efficient water-conservation method.

A swale refers to a flat or slightly inclined channel, or ditch, populated with plants, created to control water drainage, clean impurities, and boost the absorption of rainwater. Swales are usually employed to handle water drainage, eliminate contaminants, and augment rainwater seepage. The idea of the swale was first introduced by Bill Mollison, the individual credited with establishing permaculture. The swale is used to help keep the water on the land longer so that it can infiltrate into the soil and be utilized by plants.

The rainwater is captured on the uphill side of a swale and is then soaked into the ground on the downhill side of the swale. The water then slowly moves through the soil nourishing the plants and filling up the aquifer. Swales can be designed to fit the scale of your landscape and can be an effective tool for managing stormwater runoff in a sustainable way.

Many homeowners, especially those living in urban areas, may not have heard about the swale. However, it is an effective and low-cost method of controlling rainwater runoff and preventing soil erosion.

CONCLUSION

In the journey of landscape preservation, this chapter has explored the significance of preserving water flow and preventing wastage, introducing you to the concept of rainwater harvesting. The discussion traversed the fundamentals, history, and importance of this practice and laid out ways to design rainwater-harvesting systems. You discovered various components and techniques that aid in maximizing water collection from the heavens. By observing, mapping, and calculating rainfall and runoff, you are now empowered to assess your property's water-harvesting potential. Additionally, conservatory earthworks such as berms, swales, sunken beds, and waffle gardens were discussed as means of managing runoff effectively and preserving water.

Emphasizing the idea that every drop counts, the chapter's interactive element guides you to create your own DIY rainwater-harvesting system, advocating for a more self-reliant and sustainable water-management approach. As we understand the importance of securing water during rainy periods, the narrative transitions into designing water-wise irrigation practices to ensure efficient use of resources in your garden and lawn during less rainy times.

8

WATER-WISE IRRIGATION

Water, an irreplaceable source of life and the very wellspring of nature's bounty, has perhaps never been more beautifully captured than in the words of Charles Mackay (2023), who eloquently stated, "For water is the mother of the vine, The nurse and fountain of fecundity, The adorner, and refresher of the world." Water, with its vital role in the life cycle of all living things, including our cherished landscapes, is a resource we need to conserve and use judiciously. That dear reader, brings us to the crux of our conversation in this chapter: water-wise irrigation.

As we delve into this chapter, we embark on a journey of discovery—a discovery of innovative, water-efficient techniques that help us sustain our landscapes, especially under the arduous conditions of drought and water scarcity. As we traverse the rugged terrain of dry conditions, we will arm you with an arsenal of irrigation techniques to minimize water waste. In this landscape, remember, every drop saved is a triumph in itself!

But before we explore these techniques, let's take a pause to address a critical aspect— the installation of irrigation systems. While the idea of taking matters into your own hands may seem tempting, it is highly recommended to involve professionals in this process. Not only does this ensure the effective implementation of these systems, but it also helps avoid potential pitfalls that might arise from inexperienced handling.

From the basic tenets of irrigating your landscape to the nuances of automatic irrigation systems, this chapter promises to be a veritable treasure trove of valuable insights. You'll learn the merits of watering deeper and less often, understand the benefits of aiming at the base of your plants instead of their foliage, and unravel the mystery of the ideal times for irrigation.

And what's more, we also look at how to prioritize watering needs. Whether it's the towering trees that grace your garden or the vibrant flower beds that add a splash of color to your landscape, the nourishing vegetable plots or the fruitful orchards, even the ubiquitous lawns that cover the land in a lush green carpet—every component of your landscape has its unique watering needs, and we'll help you understand and cater to each one.

However, it's not just about knowing the techniques; it's also about learning to adapt and improve them based on your landscape's changing needs. For instance, how does the design of your irrigation system affect its efficiency? What are the maintenance practices that can meet the evolving water needs of your plants?

This chapter will not only equip you with practical knowledge but will also inspire you with even more ideas to create a water-wise irrigation system, from installing drip systems and using smart controllers for sprinklers to switching to more water-efficient grass varieties and covering the bare ground with mulches.

As we explore these strategies, we will also take a detour to walk you through a DIY drip-irrigation installation. However, remember, as much as we encourage you to explore, it is always best to consult professionals before attempting any installations.

By the end of this chapter, you will not only be well-versed in water-wise irrigation techniques, but you will also have taken a huge stride toward becoming a true steward of the environment. So, let's begin this exciting journey of transforming our landscapes into more water-efficient habitats, one drop at a time.

Finally, let's take a look at how you can maintain your drought-tolerant landscape to further improve water conservation and preservation.

IRRIGATING YOUR LANDSCAPE

Irrigation is a crucial part of landscape management. When done properly, it not only helps maintain healthy and vibrant gardens, but it can also significantly conserve water, an essential and limited resource. The following guidelines can help you use irrigation techniques more effectively and efficiently.

Water Deeper but Less Often

The idea behind this technique is to encourage plant roots to grow deeper, which helps plants to better withstand dry periods. Watering deeply means watering until the moisture reaches the root zone of your plants. A quick, shallow watering will merely wet the soil surface and fail to benefit your plants in the long run. On the other hand, less frequent watering prevents waterlogging and allows the soil to dry out between watering, promoting the healthier growth of plants.

Avoid the Foliage

To help prevent the spread of leaf diseases and to save water, it's essential to aim your water at the base of the plant. Watering the foliage can lead to leaf scorching, fungal diseases, and unnecessary water loss through evaporation. So, make sure you're delivering water where it counts—the roots.

Minimizing water loss due to evaporation can be achieved by watering plants during the early morning or late evening. During the heat of the day, a significant portion of the water can evaporate before it even reaches your plants. By watering when temperatures are lower, you ensure more water reaches the root zone and that your plants can utilize it better.

Automatic Irrigation Systems

These systems offer a hands-off approach to watering. They save time, reduce water waste, and can even improve plant health by providing consistent moisture. There are three main types:

Soaker Hoses

Soaker hoses are porous hoses that slowly release water along their length into the soil. They are simple to use, cheap, and can be moved easily around the garden.

Advantages

- are ideal for small gardens or those with a lot of ground-level plants
- can provide a steady amount of water over a long area
- assist in minimizing water evaporation by directing water directly to the roots

Disadvantages

- are not suitable for larger gardens or those with a lot of tall plants as it waters at ground level
- may not provide uniform watering if the water pressure is too low or if the hose is too long

Sprinkler Systems

Sprinkler systems are automated watering systems that can cover a large area. They are often used for lawns but can also be used for flower beds and other large areas.

Advantages

- cover large areas
- can be automated to water at specific times and days, reducing the effort needed

Disadvantages

- are more expensive to install and maintain
- can waste water if not correctly adjusted and maintained
- may not be suitable for certain types of plants that don't like water on their leaves

Drip Irrigation

Drip irrigation is a method that efficiently delivers water precisely to the plant's base, targeting the area where it is most needed. This system uses a network of tubes and emitters to drip water slowly into the soil at the root zone.

Advantages

- is a highly efficient use of water, ideal for water conservation
- reduces weed growth as the areas between plants remain dry
- minimizes fungal diseases by keeping foliage dry

Disadvantages

- is more expensive to install than soaker hoses
- requires regular maintenance to check for clogs and leaks
- can be unsightly if not well concealed

Water Wisely and Efficiently

When watering, it's essential to consider the type of plants, the soil conditions, the weather, and the time of year. For instance, most plants need less water in the early spring and fall than they do in the hot summer months. Also, different plants have different water needs, and these needs can change depending on their growth stage. For example, a newly planted tree will need more frequent watering than a mature one but less water at each watering.

Prioritizing Watering Needs

Different parts of your garden will have different watering needs. Here's a quick guide:

Trees

Mature trees generally need deep but infrequent watering. Water should reach a depth of 12–15 in. below the soil surface to encourage deep root growth (UOC, n.d.).

Flower Gardens

Flowers vary widely in their watering needs. Some require regular watering while others are drought tolerant. Generally, flower beds should be watered when the top 1–2 in. if soil is dry (Jauron & Klein, 2012).

Vegetable Gardens

Vegetables generally require regular and consistent watering. The soil should remain consistently moist but not waterlogged.

Fruit Gardens

Like vegetables, fruit trees and bushes usually require regular, deep watering. The top few inches of soil can dry out between watering, but the deeper soil should remain moist.

Watering the Lawn

The watering needs for your lawn can vary depending on the grass type and weather conditions. As a general guideline, the majority of lawns typically need approximately 1 in. of water per week, which can be sourced from rainfall or irrigation. Watering should be done in the early morning to minimize evaporation.

Lawns—January to June Care

During these months, it's important to prepare your lawn for the hot summer ahead. Start watering your lawn as the weather warms up and the grass starts growing. Be sure to adjust your watering based on rainfall to prevent overwatering.

Improving your irrigation management involves regularly checking your irrigation systems for leaks and clogs, adjusting your watering schedules as needed, and making sure you're watering each part of your garden appropriately.

Design of Irrigation System Affects Efficiency

The design of your irrigation system can significantly impact its efficiency. A well-designed system will deliver the right amount of water to the right places, minimizing water waste. This involves considering factors such as the water needs of different plants, the size and shape of your garden, and the water pressure.

Regular maintenance of your irrigation system is crucial to ensure it remains efficient and effective. This involves regularly checking for leaks and clogs, adjusting the system as necessary to accommodate changes in plant water needs (such as those due to seasonal changes or plant growth), and replacing any broken components.

In a nutshell, irrigation plays a pivotal role in landscaping. Efficient irrigation systems and techniques can not only help maintain healthy and vibrant landscapes but can also save water and contribute to the conservation of this essential resource. Mulches also suppress weed growth and improve soil health. Applying a 2–3 in. layer of organic mulch around plants and over bare soil can reduce irrigation needs by up to 50%.

Incorporating Smart Irrigation Controllers

Advancements in technology have provided us with smart irrigation controllers. These devices adjust watering schedules based on current weather conditions, which can be an effective way to conserve water. Smart controllers can regulate irrigation based on factors like rainfall, evaporation, and transpiration rates, thereby avoiding unnecessary watering.

Pressure Management

Too much or too little pressure can negatively impact your irrigation system's efficiency. Excessive pressure can cause misting, which leads to evaporation and wind drift. Low pressure may result in insufficient coverage. Using booster pumps or pressure reducers can help maintain optimal pressure levels for your irrigation system, ensuring efficient water usage.

Redesigning for Head-To-Head Coverage

Head-to-head coverage refers to the arrangement where each sprinkler head effectively sprays water to reach the adjacent heads. By adopting this approach, the sprinklers ensure that water distribution overlaps, resulting in uniform and consistent watering across the area. This promotes even coverage of irrigation. Redesigning your sprinkler system for head-to-head coverage can improve water application uniformity and reduce dry spots in your landscape.

Periodic System Checks

Regular inspection and maintenance of your irrigation system is crucial for water conservation. Issues like plugged screens, broken or misaligned sprinkler heads, blocked spray patterns, wind drift, and pressure problems can all lead to water wastage. Keep an eye out for these problems and promptly address them to ensure your system operates efficiently.

Fine-Tuning Your Sprinkler System

Regular water checks can help you understand your irrigation system's efficiency and diagnose any potential issues. These checks can be carried out by either a professional or the homeowner and typically involve a catch test to determine the application rate and uniformity of your sprinklers. Based on these checks, you can create a customized watering schedule for optimal water use.

Irrigation Timing and Cycling

Effective watering schedules significantly contribute to water conservation efforts. The time, duration, and frequency of watering all impact your landscape's water consumption. Watering during early morning or late evening hours can minimize evaporation. Similarly, implementing a "cycle and soak" method, where watering occurs in short, repeated intervals, can prevent runoff and enhance water absorption.

Automatic Sprinkler Controllers

Automatic sprinkler controllers can help maintain your irrigation schedules without fail. They ensure that your landscape gets the right amount of water at the right times, thereby maximizing efficiency and reducing water waste.

Implementing these practices in your landscape will not only contribute to water conservation but will also save money and promote a healthier and more beautiful landscape. Remember, every drop of water saved counts toward a sustainable future.

INTERACTIVE ELEMENT: DIY DRIP IRRIGATION
INSTALLATION

Drip irrigation is a convenient and eco-friendly way to water your garden, and installing a system in your backyard might be easier than you think. However, please always consult professionals when undertaking a project of this scale to avoid unforeseen problems. With a bit of planning and a few simple steps, you can ensure that your garden stays lush and healthy with minimal effort.

Step 1: Draw an Irrigation Plan

To begin, craft a visual representation of your yard or garden layout. Clearly mark the positions of faucets, plants, shrubs, and trees on the map. Think about which types of tubing you'll need. For example, ½ in. or ¾ in. tubing carries a larger water volume to your garden beds. You could also use soaker hoses or pre-drilled tubing for densely packed beds or large shrubs and trees. For larger trees that need more water, consider looping tubing with emitters every 6 or 12 in. around the tree.

Step 2: Gather Your Materials

Common elements for a trickle irrigation system entail tubing of ½ and ¼ in., a variety of barbed connectors, water deliverers and minuscule sprayers, spikes to secure the tubing, a tool to make holes, trimming scissors, a schedule keeper, a chief assembly with a device to prevent reverse flow, a pressure moderator, a hose connector, and a double outlet for your external tap. Arranging your components will promote a streamlined and productive operation.

Step 3: Start at the Water Source

Attach a dual outlet to your exterior tap hose bib, enabling the water to be distributed from its origin. You'll also require a main assembly incorporating a backflow filter, a pressure moderator, and a hose connector. An automatic schedule keeper can regulate the irrigation process and even provide for rainy conditions with a "weather delay" option.

Step 4: Lay the Main Tubing

Lay ½ in. tubing along the entire garden bed. For larger gardens, you might need a tee junction to split the water flow in different directions. Try to keep the total length of the tubing to about 200 ft per zone to ensure sufficient water pressure.

Step 5: Add Offshoot Tubing

Using a hole-punch tool, you can create openings in the main line to add ¼ in. offshoots that direct water to individual plants. Barbed connectors can facilitate this process, and goof plugs are available if you make a mistake.

Step 6: Install Emitters

Emitters direct water to each plant and come in various designs suitable for different water needs. Modifiable emitters offer the flexibility to adjust the drip rate, ranging from 0–10 gal per hour, allowing precise control over the water flow for efficient irrigation.

Step 7: Verify the System

Before concealing the tubing with mulch, activate the system to inspect for any leaks. In case you detect leaks, be sure to tighten the connections appropriately.

Step 8: Cover the Tubing

Once you're sure everything is working correctly, you can cover the tubing with mulch. In addition to providing concealment, using mulch also helps maintain the water's coolness during hot months. Ensure that the emitters remain uncovered by mulch and position the tubing close enough to the surface for convenient adjustments, allowing easy access to the system for necessary changes.

Your DIY drip irrigation system is now in place! You can look forward to a flourishing garden without the high water bills or the time-consuming chore of manual watering. Enjoy your beautiful plants and flowers all summer long!

CONCLUSION

As we conclude Chapter 8, it's clear that water-wise irrigation techniques are pivotal in managing dry and drought conditions effectively. Through smart watering practices, you can nourish your landscape and minimize water waste. We've explored a range of irrigation techniques, from soaker hoses and sprinkler systems to drip irrigation, each with its unique benefits and drawbacks. Furthermore, optimizing your water usage by prioritizing watering needs according to the specific requirements of different plant types in your garden can significantly enhance the effectiveness of your irrigation practices. Despite these methods being labor intensive, the results are often rewarding. Therefore, it's crucial to engage professionals when installing these systems.

Remember, nurturing Earth begins with each one of us, and adopting water-wise irrigation methods is one of many steps we can take to ensure a thriving environment. As we venture into the next chapter, we'll delve further into maintaining your drought-tolerant landscape, taking us one step closer to achieving sustainable, water-efficient gardening.

9

LANDSCAPE-MANAGEMENT PRACTICES

Picture this. It's a balmy weekend morning. The sun is just starting to dust the world with golden warmth, birds are busy orchestrating their morning symphony, and you've got a steaming mug of coffee in your hands as you survey the fruits of your labor—your carefully curated landscape. Its pristine beauty is reflected in the morning dew, an oasis in the making.

It's a picture-perfect moment, except for one nagging thought at the back of your mind: Your cherished landscape, for all its beauty, is also a voracious consumer of one of our most precious resources—water. As a conscious gardener, you understand the importance of water conservation. But how do you reconcile this need with the demand of maintaining a lush, beautiful landscape?

This chapter, dear reader, is your guide to finding that harmony. It introduces you to the 13 crucial steps for implementing best management practices (BMPs) in your landscape

—practices that not only optimize water use but also ensure the health and beauty of your plants, even in the face of severe drought. It's like a cheat sheet for your landscape management, blending aesthetics with sustainability and enabling you to make the most of every drop of water.

Just imagine tucking in your woody ornamentals and herbaceous perennials for the winter, secure in the knowledge that your meticulous planting and preparation will yield robust growth come spring. Imagine understanding your landscape's unique fertility needs, skipping the overfertilization misstep that many unknowingly fall into, and instead nurturing a vibrant ecosystem beneath the soil surface.

Or consider the satisfaction of being in tune with your landscape's irrigation needs, knowing precisely when and how much to water. Not only does this optimize water usage, but it also encourages the growth of strong, healthy root systems, the bedrock of a thriving landscape.

Moreover, this chapter also provides valuable insights into pest and disease management. You will find accessible resources and easy-to-understand tables that simplify the process of managing common problems and natural enemies within your landscape, arming you with the knowledge to keep your little slice of nature flourishing while also maintaining an ecological balance.

The information, recommendations, and resources in this chapter have been meticulously compiled to ensure you have the best, most accurate, and practical guidance at your fingertips. Let's embark on this journey together, turning the dream of a water-conscious, stunning landscape into a vivid reality.

After all, each droplet saved is a step toward a sustainable future, and it all begins right in your backyard. Welcome to the future of landscape management. Welcome to water conservation. Now, let's dive in!

BEST MANAGEMENT PRACTICES FOR LANDSCAPE INSTALLATION AND MAINTENANCE

Landscape management is an intricate process that requires careful planning, effective implementation, and continuous maintenance. Proper practices not only ensure the beauty and functionality of your landscape but also contribute to water conservation, nutrient efficiency, and pest management. This extensive guide will take you through the 13 critical steps of effective landscape management.

Step 1: Developing a Knowledge Base

Building a strong knowledge base is the fundamental cornerstone of effective landscape management. It's crucial to understand the specific needs and requirements of the plants in your landscape, the local climate conditions, and the resources available for landscape management. Continuously updating this knowledge base will assist in developing strategies that cater to your landscape's needs and the environment.

Step 2: Site Assessment

Conducting a comprehensive site assessment is a fundamental step in landscape management. It involves evaluating the physical and biological characteristics of the landscape, such as soil type, nutrient availability, sunlight exposure, and water accessibility. Moreover, a site assessment helps identify potential issues such as pests or disease presence, enabling proactive management.

Step 3: Development of a Management Plan

With the knowledge base and site assessment in hand, the next step is to develop a management plan. The plan should include a detailed approach for plant selection, planting, irrigation, soil and nutrient management, mowing, and disease and pest management. The plan should also consider the prevention and management of abiotic problems, such as environmental stressors.

Step 4: Turfgrass Selection

Selecting the appropriate turfgrass species is a vital part of the management plan. The turfgrass should be suited to the local climate and soil conditions. It should also align with the purpose of the landscape, whether it's for aesthetic appeal or functional use, such as sports or recreational activities.

Step 5: Establishment, Renovation, and Repair

After selecting the appropriate turfgrass, it's time to establish the lawn. This step involves soil preparation, turfgrass seeding or sodding, and initial watering. Post-establishment, the turfgrass may require renovation or repair due to factors such as wear and tear, pest damage, or weather-induced stress. This process could involve reseeding, aeration, or other appropriate methods to restore the turfgrass.

Step 6: Irrigation and Water Management

Effective irrigation and water management are central to maintaining a healthy and vibrant landscape. It involves watering at appropriate times and quantities to prevent overwatering or underwatering. Deep watering is recommended as it encourages strong, healthy root systems. Monitoring for moisture stress symptoms can help determine when to irrigate.

Step 7: Soil and Nutrient Management

Soil and nutrient management are essential for a thriving landscape. It involves regularly testing the soil to gauge its nutrient requirements and appropriately amending it. Slow-release fertilizers can provide more even nutrient uptake, resulting in healthier plant growth. Overfertilization should be avoided, as it can harm plants and reduce water efficiency.

Step 8: Mowing

Regular mowing helps keep turfgrass healthy and attractive. The mowing height and frequency should be determined based on the specific turfgrass species, season, and the intended use of the lawn.

Step 9: Traffic Stress and Turf Cultivation

Turfgrass can be sensitive to traffic stress, which can result in compacted soil and damaged grass. Measures such as aeration can be employed to alleviate soil compaction and encourage healthy turfgrass growth. Cultivation practices such as dethatching may also be necessary, depending on the turfgrass type and condition.

Step 10: Weed Management

Weeds can compete with desired plants for resources and potentially introduce diseases or pests. Therefore, a sound weed-management plan, including both preventive and control measures, is crucial. This might involve practices like regular weeding, the use of pre-emergent and post-emergent herbicides, or the application of mulch to prevent weed growth.

Step 11: Insect Management

Insect pests can pose a significant threat to landscape health and aesthetics. A proactive insect-management plan should be in place to monitor for pest presence, identify potential threats, and implement control measures as needed. This might involve biological control methods, the use of insecticides, or cultural practices to reduce pest populations.

Step 12: Disease Management

Like insect pests, diseases can significantly impact landscape health. A disease-management plan should include regular monitoring for disease symptoms, accurate disease identification, and the implementation of control measures. These might involve the use of fungicides, alteration of irrigation practices, or removal and disposal of infected plant material.

Step 13: Management of Abiotic Problems

Abiotic problems, such as those related to climate, soil conditions, or human activity, can negatively impact landscape health. Identifying potential abiotic stressors and implementing strategies to manage them is an essential part of landscape management. This could involve adjusting irrigation practices during drought, amending soil conditions, or managing traffic on the turfgrass.

CRUCIAL STEPS FOR LANDSCAPE MANAGEMENT

Landscape management requires a careful and thought-out approach to maximize the aesthetic value and environmental contribution of your green space. Implementing these 12 essential steps will not only enhance the beauty of your landscape but also ensure the overall health and longevity of your plants.

Autumn and Winter Sowing of Woody Decoratives and Hardy Perennials

Setting woody decorative plants and hardy perennials during the autumn and winter seasons is optimal due to the combination of cooler temperatures and abundant precipitation, which can stimulate root growth. This timing ensures your plants have a firm foundation and are primed for sprouting when spring arrives.

Adequate Preparation of the Plant Bed

The environment where your plants grow is pivotal to their survival. Tilling deeply to a depth of 8–12 in. aerates the soil, promoting healthier, deeper root systems and enhancing water drainage.

Suitable Enhancements to the Plant Bed

Enhancements can improve the physical characteristics of your soil, which can greatly influence plant vitality. The appropriate enhancements for your soil kind may comprise compost, peat moss, or other organic substances, which fortify the soil's makeup and boost its ability to retain water and nutrients.

Avoiding the Use of All-Purpose Granular Fertilizers in the Planting Hole

Fertilizers can be advantageous, but depositing all-purpose granular fertilizers directly in the planting hole can potentially harm your new plants. The concentrated nutrients can injure fragile root tissues, stalling establishment and potentially inflicting long-lasting damage.

Special Care for Seasonal Color Beds

Seasonal color beds are the stars of your landscape, drawing eyes with their vibrant hues. These beds often require extra care, including appropriate plant selection, timely planting, frequent watering, and regular fertilizing to ensure a brilliant display.

Monitoring for Moisture Stress Symptoms

Instead of sticking to a rigid watering schedule, observe your plants for signs of moisture stress, such as wilting or color change. This practice ensures that you're providing water based on your plants' actual needs, promoting healthier growth.

Night or Early Morning Irrigation

The best times to water are at night or early in the morning. Watering at these times reduces evaporation, ensuring more water reaches your plants' roots and conserving this precious resource.

Deep-Watering Practices

Deep watering encourages strong, healthy root systems. By soaking the soil thoroughly, you ensure water reaches deep into the ground, encouraging roots to grow deep as well, resulting in more resilient plants.

Soil Testing

To accurately ascertain the fertilization requirements of your landscape, conducting a soil test is considered the most effective method. It can provide vital information about nutrient deficiencies and pH imbalances in your soil, helping you make informed fertilization decisions.

Use of Slow-Release Fertilizers

Slow-release fertilizers provide nutrients over an extended period, promoting more even nutrient uptake. This method can lead to healthier plant growth and reduces the risk of nutrient leaching, protecting water resources.

While fertilizers can help plants thrive, too much of a good thing can be harmful. Overfertilization can lead to excessive growth, nutrient imbalances, and even plant death. Carefully following package directions can prevent these issues.

Refrain From Fertilizing During Dry Periods

Applying fertilizer during periods of limited rainfall can cause harm. Without sufficient water, plants can't properly absorb and utilize the nutrients, and the risk of fertilizer burn increases.

Cutting Back During Drought

During times of severe drought, it can be beneficial to cut back annual and perennial flowers. This practice can help plants conserve resources and increase their chances of survival during challenging conditions.

In sum, landscape management is a dynamic process requiring careful planning, meticulous implementation, and ongoing care. These 12 steps form a strong foundation for any land-scape-management practice, ensuring your outdoor space will thrive in all seasons.

Lawn and Turf

Maintaining healthy lawns and turf involves proper watering, aeration, fertilization, and mowing. Dealing with pests, diseases, and weeds are key aspects of lawn and turf care.

Natural Enemies

These are organisms that prey on pests and help in controlling them. They include parasitic flies and wasps, predatory beetles, bugs, flies, stinging wasps, and other predators like ants, centipedes, earwigs, lacewings, praying mantises, predatory mites and thrips, snakeflies, spiders.

CONCLUSION

It's crucial to adopt an integrated pest-management approach that includes using natural enemies, choosing disease-resistant plant varieties, proper watering and fertilization, and regular monitoring for pests and diseases. This will help you maintain a healthy and lush landscape while minimizing the use of harmful chemicals.

Working Together for a Sustainable Future

Shaping the future is a task we share, and as you step toward a more sustainable life, you're in a unique position to spread the word and get more people involved.

Simply by sharing your honest opinion of this book and a little about your own journey, you'll inspire new readers to join us on our quest to make the world a more sustainable place.

LEAVE A REVIEW!

Thank you so much for your support. For true and lasting change, we must all work together.

CONCLUSION

Standing at the precipice of this transformative journey, we find ourselves in possession of an expanded understanding, a refined mindset, and a renewed sense of purpose. In our pursuit of a more sustainable and eco-friendly way of living, we have traversed through the pages of this book, unraveling the secrets to designing and cultivating a landscape that exists in harmony with Mother Nature. The goal was not just to infuse beauty into the spaces we inhabit but to instill sustainability, foster biodiversity, and promote ecological balance.

Our journey was guided by the 3-P approach—prepare, plant, and preserve. This holistic and hands-on approach has been the guiding light throughout this book, reflecting in each chapter, each concept, and every piece of practical advice we have explored. It is the blueprint for creating, nurturing, and maintaining a landscape that reflects not only the beauty of nature but our inherent responsibility toward it.

First, we understood the power of "prepare." We came to terms with the imperative of setting a clear and conscious intent before we embarked on our transformative journey. Purpose ignited our motivation, focused our efforts, and guided our choices, reminding us constantly that we are part of a greater ecosystem. Our gardens, landscapes, or farms are not solitary islands. They are integral threads in the vast, interconnected web of life, and our purpose was to ensure their coexistence and coevolution with it.

Then came "plant." Just as a seed gives rise to a mighty tree, our mindful act of planting sets the foundation for our sustainable haven. This phase introduced us to the art and science of selecting the right plants for our spaces, understanding their affinity with the soil, ensuring appropriate water management, and so much more. The act of planting was more than just placing a seed in the ground—it was a commitment to nature, helping us turn our purpose into tangible, thriving ecosystems.

Finally, we moved into "preserve," the phase where intent met action. We dove into the nitty-gritty of sustainable landscaping, learning and implementing techniques that would help us nurture our spaces into thriving, sustainable habitats. Composting, rainwater harvesting, companion planting, and natural pest management, to name a few, brought us closer to our vision.

In following the 3-P approach, we did not just create landscapes, but we laid the foundation for a new lifestyle, one that holds the potential to ripple out into a wider social change. This book has echoed countless success stories, providing living examples of how this transformative journey is not just a personal endeavor but a communal revolution. We delved into tales of urban gardens turning concrete jungles into green havens, rural farms becoming beacons of biodiversity, and regular households transforming their yards into vibrant ecosystems. These stories stand as a testament to the power and promise of the 3-P approach, a testament to our potential to be the change we wish to see in the world.

Our journey does not end here, for the landscape of learning is ever evolving, and so must our engagement with it. Having delved deep into the nuances of sustainable landscaping and having equipped ourselves with the 3 Ps—prepare, plant, and preserve—we are now standing at the dawn of our own stories. We have armed ourselves with knowledge and understanding, and now it's time to wield these tools in the service of our environment.

Transforming our landscapes and cultivating sustainable habitats is a journey that extends beyond the physical boundaries of our gardens or farms. It's a journey that begins within us, driven by the simple yet profound choice to live in harmony with nature. The path may be dotted with challenges and surprises, but it is also filled with immense satisfaction and joy, with the magic of witnessing life thrive around us and the contentment of knowing that we played our part in nurturing it.

So, step forward. Look around. Embrace your space. And remember, the seeds you sow today will be the forests of tomorrow. Your time to make a difference starts now. Your moment to shape the landscape of the future is here. You are now equipped with the essential tools and insights to transform your landscape into a thriving and sustainable haven. It's time to put your newfound knowledge into action. Embark on your journey. Shape your story. And remember every choice, every step, every action counts. Because sustainable living is not just about doing less harm, it's about doing more good.

Your landscape awaits. Your journey begins. The future is yours to shape.

REFERENCES

Amy. (2014, February 21). *How to build a swale in the residential landscape (+ Free Download)*. Tenth Acre Farm. https://www.tenthacrefarm.com/how-to-build-swale/

Andrew "Drew" Jeffers. (2018). *Soil texture analysis "the jar test."* Home & Garden Information Center. https://hgic.clemson.edu/factsheet/soil-texture-analysis-the-jar-test/

Barrett, T. (2018, August 8). *Saving water through hydrozoning*. Ohio Irrigation Association. https://ohioia.com/news/saving-water-through-hydrozoning/

Center for Agriculture, Food, and the Environment. (2015a, March 6). *Soil tests—sampling and interpreting the results of greenhouse soil tests*. University of Massachusetts Amherst. https://ag.umass.edu/greenhouse-floriculture/fact-sheets/soil-tests-sampling-interpreting-results-of-greenhouse-soil

Center for Agriculture, Food, and the Environment. (2015b, April 13). *Soil testing*. University of Massachusetts Amherst. https://ag.umass.edu/greenhouse-floriculture/greenhouse-best-management-practices-bmp-manual/soil-testing

Crawford, B., & Cabrera, R. (2021, July.). *FS099: Problems with over-mulching trees and shrubs*. Rutgers New Jersey Agricultural Experiment Station. Njaes.rutgers.edu. https://njaes.rutgers.edu/fs099/

Elizabeth Oakes Smith quotes and sayings. (2016, June 7). *Inspiring Quotes*. https://www.inspiringquotes.us/author/8275-elizabeth-oakes-smith

Food and Agriculture Organization of the United Nations. (n.d.-a). *Saline soils and their management*. https://www.fao.org/3/x5871e/x5871e04.htm

Food and Agriculture Organization of the United Nations. (n.d.-b). *Soil texture*. https://www.fao.org/fishery/docs/CDrom/FAO_Training/FAO_Training/General/x6706e/x6706e06.htm

Goldsmith, O. (2008). *Poems and plays of Oliver Goldsmith*. https://quod.lib.umich.edu/e/ecco/004771299.0001.000/67:5.9?page=root

Jauron, R., & Klein, W. (2012, June 28). *Yard and garden: Watering plants*. Iowa State University Extension and Outreach. https://www.extension.iastate.edu/news/yard-and-garden-watering-plants

John Denham quotes. (n.d.). *"When any great design thou dost intend, Think on the means, the manner, and the end."* Quotefancy https://quotefancy.com/quote/1566132/John-Denham-When-any-great-design-thou-dost-intend-Think-on-the-means-the-manner-and-the

Kerpen, Dave. "Inc.com." Inc.com. Last modified February 26, 2014. https://www.inc.com/dave-kerpen/11-powerful-quotes-to-inspire-your-team-to-embrace-change.html.

Lent, J. (2021, February 16). *What does an ecological civilization look like? Yes!* Magazine. https://www.yesmagazine.org/issue/ecological-civilization/2021/02/16/what-does-ecological-civilization-look-like

Mackay, C. (2023). *The poetical works.* Books on Demand. https://books.google.com.pk/books?id=UenFEAAAQBAJ&pg=RA1-PA66&lpg=RA1-PA66&dq=%E2%80%9CFor+water+is+the+mother+of+the+vine

The role of rainwater harvesting in sustainable water management. (2021, September 1). Kingspan. https://www.kingspan.com/ie/en/knowledge-articles/rainwater-harvesting-for-water-conservation/

Thomas Tusser quotes. (n.d.). *"If a garden recquire it, now trench it ye may, one trench not a yard, from another go lay; Which being well filled with m...".* Quotefancy. https://quotefancy.com/quote/1450560/Thomas-Tusser-If-a-garden-require-it-now-trench-it-ye-may-one-trench-not-a-yard-from

Tiwari, S. (2020, April 18). *Mulching Meaning—Types and usage.* Agriculture Wale. https://www.agriculturewale.com/mulching-meaning-types-usage/

United Nations. (2023). Sustainability. *United Nations.* https://www.un.org/en/academic-impact/sustainability

UOC. (n.d.). *Community Forest Advisory Board City of San Diego tree preservation and watering under drought conditions.* https://ccuh.ucdavis.edu/sites/g/files/dgvnsk1376/files/inline-files/Tree%20Watering%20Handouts.pdf

USDA. (2020). *USDA plant hardiness zone map.* https://planthardiness.ars.usda.gov/

Printed in Great Britain
by Amazon

43793874R00096